"*Rewire Your Anxious Brain for Teens* is an exce[...] want to conquer anxiety. Packed with useful to[...] it brings together the best of cognitive behavio[...] ence, and mindfulness in a clearly written, comprehensive workbook. Read this book, practice the strategies within, and you *will* rewire your brain!"

> —**Kevin L. Gyoerkoe, PsyD**, director of The Anxiety and
> OCD Treatment Center in Charlotte, NC; and coauthor of
> *10 Simple Solutions to Worry*

"For teens experiencing the challenge of anxiety, this book is a treasure trove of valuable tools, presented in an effective and easy-to-understand style.

What makes this book especially valuable for teens is the format: the reader is prompted and encouraged to bring powerful tools on board through specific exercises, many of which take only a few minutes.
Specific tools empower the reader to:
- understand and befriend the experience of anxiety
- become a 'positive coach' for oneself
- practice mindfulness and meditation
- build resilience
- learn to 'dial down' intense emotions
- overcome procrastination
- enhance one's ability to focus and to move toward fulfilling goals
- overcome social anxiety"

> —**Neal Sideman**, self-help advocate, internationally known
> coach and teacher for people recovering from anxiety disorder,
> member of the Anxiety and Depression Association of America
> (ADAA) and cochair of the ADAA Public Education Committee

"*Rewire Your Anxious Brain for Teens* is a refreshing approach to helping young people understand anxiety and how to master it. By often offering two examples of teens with anxiety at a time, the reader is able to clearly see the difference between skillful and unskillful approaches to anxiety. Rather than talk down to teens, the authors appeal to teen skepticism with credible reasoning backed by science. The book is full of practical see-for-yourself exercises with easy-to-understand explanations of how these new skills literally impact the brain. I learned a lot that I wish I had known when I was a teenager."

—**Jon Hershfield, MFT**, director of The OCD and Anxiety Center of Greater Baltimore, and author of *When a Family Member Has OCD* and *Overcoming Harm OCD*

"As I read the book, I automatically thought of many of my own patients who could benefit from the exercises and examples presented in it. The exercises show young people how to relieve themselves of negative and futile self-judgments. Instead, alternatives are offered to guide a teen on an optimistic, self-directed journey toward mastery of troubling anxiety by literally 'rewiring' an anxious brain. Most teens will easily be able to see themselves in the examples, and gain a more realistic understanding of anxiety. They will also see that following the exercises will ultimately result in greater self-esteem."

—**Judith T. Davis, PhD**, president of Performance Development Associates, and psychologist in private practice

"This book was truly a pleasure to read. The authors did a tremendous job of explaining the relationship between the brain and anxiety in very user-friendly language. The inclusion of exercises throughout the book provided a hands-on opportunity to begin using the strategies discussed. I would highly recommend this book."

—**Brian J. Schmaus, PhD**, clinical psychologist at the
Anxiety Treatment Center of Greater Chicago

"There are many good informational sources to help teens decrease stress, worries, and anxiety. This one stands apart in its recognition that habitual trouble with anxiety resides in the ways your brain seeks to protect you, rather than some flaw in your personality or being. It also stands out for its creation of ten simple and specific ways you can retrain your brain, much as you might use specific exercises to retrain your abdominal muscles. If you're looking for a guide which offers CBT exercises to coach you to a path of less anxiety, here it is!"

—**David Carbonell, PhD**, author of *Panic Attacks Workbook*,
The Worry Trick, *Fear of Flying Workbook*, and
Outsmart Your Anxious Brain

"Researchers know more about the processes that produce anxiety disorders in the human brain than they do about any other disorders. This should be the best news for teens suffering from anxiety disorders, but the problem is, can the average teenage anxiety sufferer *understand* the brain processes that need to be changed in order to overcome an anxiety disorder? Based on over one hundred combined years of working with anxious teens, these authors have put together an amazing book that not only explains the anxious brain in language a teen can understand, but also provides exercises and strategies that give teens the resources they need to change their brains in order to have needed control over their anxiety. With clear examples and explanations, the book pulls readers in, preparing them to engage in the process of taking charge of their lives. This book is a dream come true for anxious teens and the therapists who help them. It will change millions of lives."

> —**Catherine M. Pittman, PhD, HSPP**, coauthor of *Rewire Your Anxious Brain*, and professor in the department of psychology at Saint Mary's College in Notre Dame, IN

the *i*nstant help
solutions series

Young people today need mental health resources more than ever. That's why New Harbinger created the **Instant Help Solutions Series** especially for teens. Written by leading psychologists, physicians, and professionals, these evidence-based self-help books offer practical tips and strategies for dealing with a variety of mental health issues and life challenges teens face, such as depression, anxiety, bullying, eating disorders, trauma, and self-esteem problems.

Studies have shown that young people who learn healthy coping skills early on are better able to navigate problems later in life. Engaging and easy-to-use, these books provide teens with the tools they need to thrive—at home, at school, and on into adulthood.

This series is part of the **New Harbinger Instant Help Books** imprint, founded by renowned child psychologist Lawrence Shapiro. For a complete list of books in this series, visit newharbinger.com.

rewire your anxious brain
for teens

using cbt, neuroscience & mindfulness to help you end anxiety, panic & worry

DEBRA KISSEN, PhD
ASHLEY D. KENDALL, PhD
MICHELLE LOZANO, LMFT
MICAH IOFFE, PhD

Instant Help Books
An Imprint of New Harbinger Publications, Inc.

Publisher's Note

NEW HARBINGER PUBLICATIONS is a
registered trademark of New Harbinger Publications, Inc.

Distributed in Canada by Raincoast Books

Copyright © 2020 by Debra Kissen, Ashley D. Kendall, Michelle Lozano, and Micah Ioffe
Instant Help Books
An imprint of New Harbinger Publications, Inc.
5674 Shattuck Avenue
Oakland, CA 94609
www.newharbinger.com

Cover design by Amy Shoup; Acquired by Tesilya Hanauer; Edited by Karen Schader

Library of Congress Cataloging-in-Publication Data

Names: Kissen, Debra, author.
Title: Rewire your anxious brain for teens : using CBT, neuroscience, and mindfulness to help you end anxiety, panic, and worry / Debra Kissen, Ashley D. Kendall, Michelle Lozano, and Micah Ioffe.
Description: Oakland, CA : New Harbinger Publications, [2020] | Series: The instant help solutions series | Includes bibliographical references.
Identifiers: LCCN 2019055192 (print) | LCCN 2019055193 (ebook) | ISBN 978168403 3768 (paperback) | ISBN 9781684033775 (pdf) | ISBN 9781684033782 (epub)
Subjects: LCSH: Anxiety in adolescence--Juvenile literature. | Cognitive therapy for teenagers--Juvenile literature. | Mindfulness-based cognitive therapy--Juvenile literature.
Classification: LCC RJ506.A58 K53 2020 (print) | LCC RJ506.A58 (ebook) | DDC 618.92/8522--dc23
LC record available at https://lccn.loc.gov/2019055192
LC ebook record available at https://lccn.loc.gov/2019055193

Printed in the United States of America

24   23   22

10   9   8   7   6   5   4   3

Contents

Letter to the Reader

We're so glad you're reading these words. You may be wanting to move past your own anxiety or find ways to support a loved one. You'll find help in these pages, as you participate in our brain rewiring training program.

We, the authors of this book, are four anxiety specialists who work together at Light on Anxiety Treatment Center, where we offer treatment for anxiety and related disorders to children, adolescents, and adults. We use treatment protocols that are supported by lots of data and research. We've helped many teens like you move past anxiety and get back to their lives. We know techniques that will assist you in harnessing your power to rewire your brain to become a less anxious, more relaxed person. We strive to make the process of moving past anxiety as efficient, effective, and—believe it or not—fun as possible.

After seeing countless teens move past anxiety and reclaim their lives, we were inspired to take our treatment model and philosophy "on the road." We wanted to reach more teens looking to rewire their brain to experience less anxiety and misery. Our little idea became bigger, and soon became the book you're now holding.

We're not only anxiety treatment specialists but also fellow humans with our own fears, insecurities, and challenges. By practicing the same concepts we'll be reviewing with you in this book, we've rewired our own brains. Daily, we recommit to continuing the work of teaching our brains to recognize anxiety when it's simply a false alarm. And we continue to practice the best ways to move forward, one step at a time, to seek out all life has to offer. We'll teach you how to do this!

This work isn't easy for us, and it won't be easy for you, but the journey is powerful and transformative. You'll soon be living your life with a greater sense of peace and satisfaction.

We are honored to join you on this journey of rewiring your brain to move through and soon past anxiety. And with these words, it's time to get started. Your life awaits you!

With tons of respect and support,

Your Brain Rewiring Trainers

Debra Kissen, PhD, MHSA

Ashley Kendell, PhD

Micah Ioffe, PhD

Michelle Lozano, LMFT

Introduction

You may believe some people are just born calm while others will spend their lives struggling with anxiety. But lucky for you (and us), this is untrue. All mental states can be strengthened through targeted mental exercises. What you're holding isn't just another self-help book; it's a training program you can use to rewire your brain to experience more peace and operate less frequently in "anxiety mode."

Even people born with great athletic abilities have to train to achieve peak performance levels. It's the same with your mind. If you want to feel cool, calm, and collected, you'll have to develop and maintain these positive mental states through brain training exercises like the ones we'll review with you. By engaging in these exercises, you'll rewire your brain to be less anxious and more engaged in meaningful living.

WELCOME TO YOUR MIND GYM

For any training plan to be successful, it has to be user-friendly and easy to implement. That's why we developed this simple-to-use program that will serve as your mind gym. It includes the ten fundamental skills you'll need to rewire your brain to experience less anxiety.

If you're taking time out of your life to read this book, it's quite likely that just seeing the word "anxiety" triggers feelings of gloom and doom. However, there's good news when it comes to struggling with an overly anxious brain. We're happy to report that anxiety is the most treatable mental health condition.

The exercises in this book are derived from cognitive behavioral therapy (CBT) treatment protocols for anxiety disorders. CBT has been proven to effectively treat anxiety symptoms and produce long-lasting change by helping you learn strategies to move past your anxious thoughts, feelings, and behaviors. And when you learn, you're rewiring and strengthening new connections in your brain.

Each chapter will help you rewire your brain to:

- recognize and disengage from anxiety when it's simply a false alarm, and realize that you're actually safe and sound;

- serve as a more supportive, encouraging coach, instead of a judgmental self-critic;

- move through and past frustrating and disappointing moments;

- move through life more flexibly;

- be more mindful and engaged in the present moment;

- manage intense, overwhelming emotions more effectively;

- do less procrastinating and avoiding;

- experience a greater sense of confidence; and

- customize your own brain rewiring program that builds on the specific exercises that best targeted your personal growth goals.

This book will share information with you through several formats. Each chapter provides you with an example of two teens who are experiencing similar anxiety-provoking situations. The chapter then highlights how one teen, "on anxiety," handles the situation and the other, operating from a more flexible and balanced mind-set, moves through the scenario. Next, you'll find a minicourse on neuroscience and the areas of the brain that are activated by anxiety—the areas we'll be targeting and rewiring to allow for more moments of calm, peaceful living. After that comes the secret sauce of this program: targeted exercises and activities that will train your brain to operate more effectively. Each chapter ends with key takeaways you can use to plan how to integrate the important lessons you've learned into your life.

Before you get started, we suggest you gather a few items and choose a work space and time to dedicate to this mind training. Planning details like these can be the difference between success and disappointment. It's like trying to meet your fitness goals. If you decide to prioritize going to the gym but haven't signed up for membership or scheduled your workouts, it's unlikely you'll succeed at meeting those goals.

BRAIN REWIRING TRAINING JOURNAL

To get the most out of the exercises offered throughout this book, we recommend you set aside a journal or notebook to be used exclusively as your brain rewiring training journal. You'll see the symbol 📓 when you need your journal. A written record of your experience with each exercise can serve as a reminder to help you get unstuck from an anxious moment.

Some teens would rather walk on hot coals than have to track their work using pen and paper. If that's you, we recommend using the notes section of your phone or creating a document on your computer to serve as your journal. You're welcome to use whatever method works best for you. The most important thing is that you're realistic with yourself: what format will make it easiest for you to consistently complete the exercises in this book and track your progress? It's also important to do these exercises in a quiet place so that you can complete them without interruption.

Throughout this book, you'll also see the icon 💻, which means that complementary worksheets are available to download at http://www.newharbinger.com/43768. You can also use these forms to help you complete the recommended exercises.

Finally, the icon ☞ points to reflection questions. Reflection questions don't require using your brain rewiring journal, and answers need not be written out. Instead, they highlight material to be thought through and considered.

MEET YOUR BRAIN: SOME BASICS

We're not asking you to become a neurologist, brain surgeon, or any other kind of brain expert, but some simple brain basics will help you further understand how to more effectively operate this complex command center for the human nervous system—aka, your wonderful, powerful, and occasionally overly charged brain.

The first critical point for you to understand is how many interdependent cells come together to create this powerful organ. Your brain is made up of hundreds of billions of neurons (or nerve cells), and each one has the capacity to connect to ten thousand other neurons. Think of your brain as an all-powerful highway—all these neurons are transmitting information at lightning speed through endless connections. For all this to take place, we need the hardware to create this information highway.

Your brain structures—mainly the prefrontal cortex, amygdala, and hippocampus—serve as this hardware. Within these structures, you have your brain's software, the many neurons that connect with many other neurons, creating the wiring of your brain. They connect by sending chemical messengers to one another. Some connections are stronger than others, and some neurons have more connections than others. These connections (or wiring) allow for communication among your brain's hardware, which then allows you to richly experience the world around you. You get to feel your feelings, think your thoughts, and take action in line with your goals and interests.

The second critical fact for you to know is that you have the power to rewire your brain to operate more effectively. Learning and experiencing anything—a shortcut to a friend's house, how to play soccer, that you don't like pickles—create new connections between the neurons in your brain. Your brain's ability to adapt and change over time is called *neuroplasticity*. Each time you think a thought or engage in a behavior, you're altering the connections between neurons in your brain. With each action you take, you're rewiring your brain to experience stronger connections in some areas and weaker connections in others. The more frequently you think and behave in particular patterns, the more likely you'll be to think and act the very same way in the future. This is because with repetition, you're strengthening the connections between the neurons associated with these specific thoughts and behaviors.

You can create new neuron connections and rewire your brain to be less anxious by *repeatedly* practicing thinking and behaving in new, more effective ways that we'll be reviewing with you throughout this book. But change can be difficult. It's easier and feels more comfortable to stick with what you know. It's kind of like a groove in a dirt road. Every time you drive over that road, the groove gets deeper and more defined. You can certainly take a different path, but it would be easier to take the more familiar route. Finding and taking a new path requires extra effort. But soon enough, this new path will also become well-worn, and eventually it will be just as easy to travel this alternate route. The same is true of rewiring your brain to become less anxious. By strengthening neural pathways associated with states of calm and peace, your brain will be more likely to travel these roads moving forward.

Your Brain's Hardware

Let's take a brief look at three key areas of the brain and how they interact to create the experience of anxiety.

Amygdala: This is your "emotional brain." The amygdala labels emotion, like love and anger, and especially the feeling of fear. Your amygdala quickly determines how it feels about something way before your more rational thinking brain has had a chance to finalize its assessment. It decides if you should approach or avoid a situation and if something is good or bad for you. It prioritizes survival over a good time and forms emotional memories that are out of your awareness. You may not understand why you're feeling afraid, but in that moment, something has captured your amygdala's attention. The amygdala learns through experience—it doesn't use logic to come to its emotional conclusions. Like a personal bodyguard, it's always on high alert, looking out for potential danger and is more likely to assume something can cause you harm than bring you joy. It's constantly reviewing new incoming data. When it detects any potential threats, it sends messages of alert to your brain and signals it to prepare for danger. You don't just hear a simple "Watch out!" from your amygdala. You *feel* the danger all throughout your body. Think of it as not only hearing the screech of a fire alarm but also seeing the red bell shaking, feeling the vibration of the ringing, and maybe even smelling something burning. Your senses are flooded with the message of danger. And in the face of potential danger, your brain is hardwired to override your more level-headed thinking brain (described below) so your amygdala can run the show and keep you out of harm's way.

Your amygdala comes with some preprogrammed fears that are advantageous on the survival front, such as fear of large animals, heights, sharp objects, and unfamiliar faces. It also learns what to approach or avoid based on your specific experiences. For example, if you are bitten by a dog, your amygdala will remember this experience and remind you to avoid similar situations in the future. Moving forward, your amygdala will try to protect you by setting off danger alarms when you encounter, or may encounter, another dog.

Your amygdala is powerful and hardworking, but it lacks in attention to detail. It doesn't ask questions like "Is this a calm dog or an out-of-control dog?" or "Does it seem like its owner trained it to be comfortable with people?" Instead, it operates on more of a Tarzan level of "Dog bad ... avoiding dog good." It remembers only the pain and suffering associated with being attacked by a dog and will continue to signal you to stay away from any doglike creatures until it learns otherwise through a positive experience. Your amygdala's rapid fear response can cause you a lot of unnecessary anxiety and get in the way of experiencing the more enjoyable aspects of life.

When your amygdala decides something is a threat, it urges you to react immediately by going into fight (defending yourself) or flight (running away) or freeze (hide and don't attract attention) mode. But being in one of these modes is extremely uncomfortable when you're actually in a safe situation that your amygdala has mistakenly classified as dangerous. In these cases, it's helpful to be able to readily access the more logical, rational part of your brain, in order to quiet down the alarm set off by your overeager amygdala. So without further ado, it's time to introduce you to your prefrontal cortex.

Prefrontal cortex (PFC): This is your "thinking brain." It uses logic and can rationally think through challenges and scenarios. The PFC is basically your planner, organizer, decision-maker, anticipator, and interpreter. It sorts through both incoming sensory input (what you see, hear, smell, taste, touch) and stored memories in order to decide how to proceed. The PFC uses this information to attach meaning to situations and store them as memories, which helps you easily recognize, interpret, and respond to people, places, and things.

Your PFC not only helps you navigate your current situation but also has the ability to review previously learned lessons and visualize future situations in order to maximize the likelihood of successful living. But sometimes its ability to picture all the possible outcomes of a future scenario hurts more than it helps and leaves your amygdala feeling overwhelmed by endless possibilities and challenges. Your PFC and your amygdala have a two-way relationship. Your PFC influences your amygdala and your amygdala influences your PFC.

The good news is that you can rewire your PFC to more effectively and efficiently calm down by practicing thinking in new ways. You can also rewire your amygdala by teaching it how to calm down when it's not facing an immediate threat, which will then help your PFC in thinking more clearly.

Hippocampus: This is your "memory storage and retrieval brain." It creates and stores short-term and long-term memories, like locations of things and places associated with different people. It especially remembers moments of high emotion in your life, both positive and negative. It's the emotion that seals in memories. Your hippocampus is constantly sharing information with your overeager amygdala to try to maximize the value of lessons you've already learned. But as you just read, your amygdala has a way of overgeneralizing past negative experiences in order to protect you against future pain and suffering. For example, your hippocampus may send a message to your amygdala: "Remember last time you tried to make plans with a new friend and they rejected you?" And your amygdala responds, "Yes, I remember. I never want to feel that awful shame and rejection again. We need to avoid taking all social risks moving forward."

As you can see, your brain is wonderfully complex. Different parts perform different critical functions, but all are in service of maximizing your chances of survival. Some areas of your brain are more primitive and similar to other mammalian brains, and some are more evolved and allow you to plan, predict, and reflect on your experience in ways that only humans can. Your more developed brain components allow you to engage in complex thinking and access unique abilities, like language. These advanced thinking and planning skills are awesome on the survival front and have allowed humans to outsmart the changing times, while stronger, faster, and fiercer animals have become extinct. The downside of having such a powerful brain is that it comes without a user manual, and it can be difficult to operate without some guidance and support. This book is here to help with that training.

WHAT MOTIVATES YOU TO DO THIS HARD WORK?

Like buying a gym membership and then having little motivation to get off the couch to go work out, just reading the exercises in this book will do you little good. It's through action, hard work, and commitment that you'll begin to see progress in the form of a less anxious brain. So let's review why you're taking time out of your busy life to engage in this training program.

Exercise #1: Who Would You Be Without Anxiety?

Useful for: Reminding yourself why you're taking the time to do this program. This material will be critical to review when the going gets tough and you're struggling to find the motivation to put in the work required to rewire your brain.

Time needed: Five to ten uninterrupted minutes

Write the answers to these questions in your journal:

- If we waved a magic wand and on the count of three ... poof ... you were no longer struggling with anxiety, how would your life look different?

- What would you be doing at this moment (besides not reading this book)?

- What activities would you be engaging in?

- Who would you be talking to and spending time with?

- What are you missing out on because of your struggles with anxiety?

Here's how one teen completed this exercise:

If I had a magic wand and could make anxiety go away, the first thing that comes to mind is that I'd be more comfortable in my own skin. If I weren't always so anxious, I'd talk to more people at school. I'd have lunch with friends instead of making excuses to go to the library. I'd participate more in class and maybe even sign up for classes I'm interested in, even if I might have to give a presentation. I'd apply for summer jobs where I could learn more about graphic design, instead of working at the pizza restaurant again. I'd spend more time doing things that may make me happy instead of spending my days reviewing options in order to determine what will be least likely to bring on anxiety. And maybe, just maybe, I'll feel a bit of peace—and to be really greedy right now, a hint of joy and pleasure would be nice as well.

How Is This Exercise Rewiring Your Brain?

Your brain needs encouragement and gentle reminders as to why it's important to tolerate a bit of discomfort as you do this rewiring work instead of choosing the easier, more familiar path of avoidance and retreating. As you move through this program, there will be times when your brain will protest against this work. At those moments, you can look back at this exercise to remind yourself of your goals and desires, and to help you visualize what your life can and will be once you move past this struggle with anxiety. In doing so, you're rewiring your PFC to be able to more clearly and concisely coach your amygdala through and past its resistance.

CHAPTER 1

Rewire Your Brain to Move Past Anxiety

Jillian and Samantha were riding the train together when they heard a commotion. Two fellow passengers had begun to argue. The argument escalated and soon both participants were yelling and getting physical. One reached into his pocket and, for a moment, it looked like he was going to pull out a weapon. Jillian and Samantha, as well as other passengers, took cover and hid under their seats. Jillian felt her heart pounding and began to sweat. She felt dizzy and her stomach felt queasy. Her thoughts were racing. All she could think about was that the situation was escalating, and that she could get hit by a stray bullet. Samantha was equally terrified. She was feeling shaky and having difficulty breathing. Her heart was pounding. She was feeling frozen in place and, at the same time, an urgent need to flee and escape from the train. Thankfully, the police soon arrived and arrested the two offenders, and the rest of the day was uneventful.

Both Samantha and Jillian tried to put the frightening train incident behind them and move on with their lives. Samantha would occasionally think about how scared she had felt and all the anxious thoughts and feelings would immediately resurface. Samantha allowed herself to have these uncomfortable feelings and understood on some intuitive level that she just needed to ride out the anxiety and eventually it would pass.

Jillian too experienced occasional flare-ups of anxiety. While she knew that her initial feelings of terror were caused by the fight, she did not understand why she was still feeling so anxious and uncomfortable in her own skin. She kept thinking about how out of control and awful she felt the day of the fight, and how desperately she hoped to never feel that scared again. Jillian began asking her parents for rides so she could avoid taking trains, and she started staying away from crowded spots. She did everything and anything she could think of to help herself feel less scared. She began to feel trapped and hopeless. It seemed the harder she worked to feel safe and eliminate anxiety from her life, the more anxious she was getting.

What's the moral of this story? Both Jillian and Samantha have experienced the same frightening event. But Jillian is reacting to her anxiety as though it's a source of danger and needs to be avoided at all costs while Samantha is relating to her anxiety as an uncomfortable but necessary part of the healing process. When Jillian responds with fear to her anxiety, she is bringing on more of the very sensations she is hoping to escape. And from there she is stuck in an ever-expanding web of anxiety about anxiety and fear of fear.

☞ *How effective are Jillian's efforts to reduce her feelings of fear and anxiety?*

☞ *Why do you think Jillian's attempts to avoid anxiety triggers and frequently check for danger are not helping her feel safer and less anxious?*

☞ *What are you currently doing to reduce your feelings of anxiety?*

☞ *What seems to help decrease your anxiety level?*

☞ *Can you think of any behaviors you are engaging in to decrease your anxiety that may actually be backfiring and serving to increase your overall anxiety?*

ANXIETY ABOUT ANXIETY INCREASES ANXIETY

Let's take a closer look at Jillian's experience. The more Jillian tried to avoid anxiety, the larger her anxiety seemed to grow. This is because anxiety feeds on avoidance. Every time you choose to forgo participating in an aspect of your life that you otherwise would enjoy in order to not feel anxious, you're giving your anxiety a supersized, protein-packed, muscle-building smoothie. Every time you retreat rather than going forward, your brain concludes, "Wow, that must have been super dangerous. Good thing we didn't just go to that party (or take that test, or ask that person out, or take that trip…)." When you rely on avoidance to decrease anxiety, your brain misses out on the opportunity to learn how to distinguish between what is a true threat and what is safe.

IT'S ONLY A FALSE ALARM

Have you ever accidentally set off a smoke detector? Perhaps you were microwaving some popcorn when suddenly a ton of smoke arose from the microwave, setting off the alarm. And thank goodness for that alarm because if there had been a real fire, you could have quickly left the premises and gotten yourself to safety. But when you're trying to make yourself an after-school snack and your relaxing moment is interrupted by the obnoxious sound of an alarm, the smoke detector is more annoying than helpful. The same thing happens when your amygdala mistakenly detects danger and sounds a full-blown anxiety alarm.

You may be sitting in class listening to your teacher when, out of nowhere, you begin to feel anxious. Something may have caught your amygdala's attention that it interpreted as dangerous. Perhaps someone sitting near you is wearing a perfume associated with a difficult time in your past, or there's a shadow from the back corner of the room that your amygdala believes may be a threat. There are endless cues that may set off your amygdala's threat-detection system. Most often, it will be difficult to know exactly what your amygdala is reacting to. But the good news is that you don't need to know what set off your amygdala in order to calm it down. You can access your PFC and have it coach your amygdala through a false alarm by calmly and compassionately pointing out that the coast is clear and that everything is okay. Some exercises will help too.

Some situations may feel dangerous in the sense that you feel rejected or like you have failed. Rejection and failure, though difficult, are not dangerous; they are experiences that are important life lessons and should not be avoided. By facing and not fleeing these moments of the human experience, you're teaching your brain that it can handle them, leading to less pain and suffering the next time around.

The amygdala is meant to help you fight, flee, or freeze when confronted with a situation where your survival is actually at risk.

Our caveman ancestors needed their amygdala to take action if their lives were threatened by a charging lion: they could attack (fight), run away (flee), or hide and be completely still in hopes of not attracting any attention to themselves (freeze). And all stressors look like a charging lion when viewed through your amygdala. When it's in check, the amygdala can actually be a powerful tool to help you manage everyday stressors, such as challenges at school or work, or in your social life. Lucky for you that you have a handy-dandy PFC that loves nothing more than distinguishing between true danger and false alarms!

📖 or 💻
Exercise #2: True Danger or False Alarm?

Useful for: Rewiring your brain to better distinguish between true danger and false alarms.

Time needed: Fifteen to twenty minutes for Parts A and B. Part C should be completed over the course of a week.

Part A: Identify whether each situation represents true danger or a false alarm.

- You're taking an important exam and begin to feel hot and flushed and have a difficult time concentrating.

- You're driving on the highway and notice that your heart rate is accelerating and your hands feel tingly.

- A fire breaks out in your home.

- A lion lunges at you.

- You're at a party with friends and begin to feel weird and out of control.

- You're about to step on a rattlesnake.

- You're walking up a flight of stairs and have trouble taking a deep breath and a tight feeling in your chest.

- You're about to give a class presentation and your mind goes blank.

Part B: Answer these questions in your journal or download the worksheet at http://www.newharbinger.com/43768:

- Think of a time when anxiety helped protect you from true danger.

- Now think of a time when anxiety was a false alarm and you weren't actually in harm's way.

- How were the thoughts, feelings, and sensations you experienced in these two scenarios similar?

- How were the thoughts, feelings, and sensations you experienced in these two scenarios different?

Part C: For the next week, keep a log of all moments when you find yourself feeling increased anxiety. You can use your journal or download a blank worksheet at http://www.newharbinger.com/43768, where you'll also see a sample entry. Write down the date and time and a few details about the situation you're in. Next, look around your immediate environment and ask yourself, *Am I in true danger, or is this a false alarm?* Finally, write down one coaching thought you can offer yourself to get through each moment that is a false alarm.

How Is This Exercise Rewiring Your Brain?

Research has shown that with the repeated practice of reminding your anxious brain that you're in a false-alarm situation and not truly in danger—and labeling it as such—you can rewire your PFC to override your amygdala's inaccurate threat signal. By doing this exercise, you're training your brain to improve its accuracy and speed when sorting between junk mail (false alarm) and priority mail (true threat).

☞ *On a scale of 1 to 10, rate how much it's a priority for you to continue to work on rewiring your brain to better distinguish between false alarms and true danger.*

ANXIETY IS YOUR GREATEST DEFENDER

We're assuming that you're currently not a member of the "I love anxiety" fan club. More likely, you view anxiety as your archenemy whose main goal is to block you from the experience of peace, pleasure, and happiness. But the reality is that anxiety is *actually on your team*. It's trying to protect you from danger. It wants nothing more than for you to survive another day and live a long, prosperous life.

When we introduce this idea to the teens we work with, they often express disbelief and say something along the lines of "With friends like anxiety, who needs enemies?" They wonder what could possibly be helpful about difficulty in breathing, a pounding heart, feeling both hot and cold at the same time, trouble concentrating and thinking clearly, and so on. The best way to answer this question is to provide a brief view of the body on anxiety.

The Body on Anxiety

In order for you to have a potential shot at outrunning a lion or fleeing from a burning building, your body needs all its available resources. Mustering up all that energy requires an increase in breathing, heart rate, and blood pressure. If you were in a true emergency, you wouldn't be aware of how your body is feeling when "on anxiety" because you'd be too busy trying to survive.

But when your amygdala is in false-alarm mode and your PFC has no external threat to capture its attention, your PFC tends to use its advanced thinking and analyzing skills to try to determine why you're feeling so awful. It's common for the PFC to conclude "Something must be wrong with me" in order to make sense of the alarming array of uncomfortable sensations happening in your body.

It can be helpful to teach your PFC the biological origin of the different sensations of anxiety so it can come to a new, informed conclusion when experiencing your amygdala's powerful and bewildering false alarm. Without this knowledge, your PFC will continue to conclude that the uncomfortable sensations of anxiety are signs that something is in fact wrong, and then your amygdala will react to this by providing you with another heaping serving of anxiety to help you survive this new threat. And round and round in the anxiety cycle you will go!

Biological Explanation of Common Anxiety Sensations

Sensation: Feeling dizzy and disconnected from reality

These sensations are due to overbreathing. When faced with an imagined threat, the body takes in excess oxygen to power up muscles to flee from danger.

Sensation: Tingly, cold hands and feet

Your hands and feet may feel tingly and cold due to blood flow being redirected from your hands and feet to muscles more critical to survival, such as your arms and legs.

Sensation: Blurred or altered vision

Your pupils may dilate in order to better perceive danger. This can make your vision extra sensitive to stimuli in your visual field.

Sensation: Foggy head or difficulty concentrating

These sensations are due to decreased blood flow to the head and increased blood flow to muscles required for survival, such as your arms and legs.

Sensation: Increased sweating

Sweating cools your body off so you don't overheat. An additional benefit is that sweat makes you slippery, so it would be difficult for an angry predator to hold on to you.

Sensation: Upset stomach

You may be feeling nauseated or experiencing other symptoms of an upset stomach due to blood flow being redirected from your digestive system to other parts of your body. After all, when you're about to be someone else's meal is no time to digest your own big meal!

Sensation: Difficulty breathing

To fuel up for battle, your body takes in extra oxygen (hyperventilates). Taking in so much oxygen and breathing out so much carbon dioxide can create a smothered feeling.

Sensation: Heart racing

In the face of danger, your heart beats faster to supply more oxygenated blood to your vital organs to fuel you up for battle.

Sensation: Feeling shaky

To assist you in escaping from danger, your body releases the hormone epinephrine (also known as adrenaline). Adrenaline directs blood to your muscles to power you up for the fight of your life. The increased blood flow to your muscles may leave you feeling shaky.

📖 or 💻
Exercise #3: Your Body on Anxiety

Useful for: Rewiring a brain to decrease its anxious reaction to anxiety sensations.

Time needed: Fifteen to twenty minutes

You'll need your journal, or you can download a worksheet (along with a completed sample) at http://www.newharbinger.com/43768.

First, jot down the anxiety sensations you tend to experience the most often. Next, write down different explanations you've told yourself about why you were feeling these strange, uncomfortable feelings; for example, *I'm going* crazy, or *I'm dying*, or *There's something wrong with me*. Finally, write out your new understanding of the biological explanation for these sensations.

How Is This Exercise Rewiring Your Brain?

This exercise helps rewire your PFC to more quickly recognize when your amygdala is experiencing a false alarm and that you're actually safe and sound. Your PFC will shift from believing that it's in danger to serving as a calm and competent coach that can help settle down your amygdala and turn off the danger signal.

In addition, by teaching your PFC what is actually happening when your body is on anxiety, you're building a neural pathway that can more efficiently and effectively communicate logical explanations for the sensations of anxiety, rather than relying on your amygdala's predictions of gloom and doom.

☞ *On a scale of 1 to 10, rate how much it's a priority for you to continue to work on rewiring your PFC to not freak out when your amygdala is in false-alarm mode and experiencing a bewildering array of uncomfortable anxiety sensations.*

ANXIOUS BUT FUNCTIONAL?

The teens we work with often share stories with us about all the things they simply "could not do" because they were too anxious. For example, one girl said she had to leave class when she felt an anxiety episode kicking in. We then challenge them by asking if they *had to* leave a situation due to anxiety or if they *chose to* leave. More often than not, they tell us that if they didn't flee, some catastrophic outcome would have occurred.

These common fears are associated with the experience of anxiety:

- I'll die.

- I'll go crazy.

- I'll faint.

- I'll say stupid things that don't make sense.

- No words will come out of my mouth.

- I'll scream or lose control in some other embarrassing way.

- My mind will go blank.

But as we've already discussed, anxiety is there to assist you in survival. If anxiety made you die, go crazy, faint, or lose control, it would be terrible at its job. Anxiety may be a trigger-happy worry-wart, but it's *not* stupid.

CHALLENGING YOUR ANXIETY ABOUT ANXIETY

Your PFC may now understand that anxiety is a natural, powerful state that is super uncomfortable to experience absent a true threat, but your amygdala is not so easily convinced of this truth. Your PFC can rewire through abstract reasoning, but your amygdala must learn through experience. If you've been struggling with anxiety for a while, chances are that at this point in the training, you're beginning to intellectually develop a new relationship with anxiety.

However, your amygdala still sees it as the enemy to be avoided or battled at all costs. And until we can teach your amygdala to give up its struggle with anxiety, you'll continue to be stuck in the cycle of anxiety → anxiety about anxiety → more anxiety.

The next brain rewiring exercises you'll be practicing will train your amygdala to get used to your anxious sensations. We'll coach you on how to intentionally bring on the sensations of anxiety, and then practice "playing" with these feelings. Yes, you read that correctly. We're going to train you on how to play with anxiety, and you're going to train your amygdala to grow stronger and fearless when anxiety sensations surface (and you're experiencing a false alarm). You will be one giant step closer to freedom from anxiety.

📖 and 💻
Exercise #4: Play with Anxiety

Useful for: Rewiring your brain to get used to anxiety sensations rather than fighting with or hiding from them.

Time needed: Twenty to thirty uninterrupted minutes daily

This exercise requires repetition for at least a week or until you grow bored with it and no longer have a fear-based reaction to the sensations of anxiety. To make it easier to achieve the benefits of this exercise, you can download the sheet at http://www.newharbinger.com/43768 and paste it into your journal.

Part A: Review the list of anxiety sensations in the column on the left. If you could eliminate the ones that bother you most, which three would you choose?

Circle the three anxiety sensations you find the most unbearable. Follow the instructions on how to engage in all the different recommended exercises that assist in bringing on feelings similar to your least favorite anxiety sensations. We recommended that you practice each exercise for one minute or for as long as it takes for your brain to grow bored with it or stop feeling anxious about the feeling.

Note: *Although these exercises are in no way dangerous, people who are actively struggling with anxiety may fear trying them. If you're feeling hesitant, we suggest you ask a friend or family member to join you in bringing on these feelings. And you never know—they might also be struggling with anxiety and these exercises may benefit them as well.*

Anxiety sensations	Exercises to bring on feeling
Foggy headed, difficulty concentrating, or light-headed	Hyperventilate for one minute (breathe loudly and rapidly, like a panting dog), taking approximately forty-five breaths per minute. Place your head between your legs for one minute, then quickly sit up.
Feeling weird and out of it	Stare up at the sky and think about the solar system and how teeny-tiny you truly are. Stare up at the sky and picture yourself standing on the earth as it rotates around the sun. Stand still in a dark room, blindfolded, with noise-canceling headphones on for five minutes. Think to yourself, *Who am I? Who am I?* over and over for five minutes.

Anxiety sensations	Exercises to bring on feeling
Distorted vision	Stare intensely at your eyes in a mirror for one minute. Stare at a spot on the wall for one minute. Put on dark glasses indoors. With your eyes open, spin rapidly in a circle for one minute. Stare at a light bulb for one minute and then try to read.
Difficulty breathing	Hold your nose and breathe through a thin straw for one minute.
Feelings of suffocation	Wrap your hands tightly around your throat. Wear a tight turtleneck. Spend one minute in a small space, such as a closet.
Increased heart rate or tightness in your chest	Drink a coffee or espresso or other caffeine-based drink. Run up and down stairs for five minutes. Do five minutes of moderately intense cardiovascular exercise.
Upset stomach	Think about something upsetting or write down upsetting thoughts for five minutes. Do twenty jumping jacks after a meal.

Anxiety sensations	Exercises to bring on feeling
Tingly, cold hands or feet	Hyperventilate for one minute (breathe loudly and rapidly, like a panting dog) at a rate of approximately forty-five breaths per minute.
Feeling shaky	Tense all your muscles and hold the tension for one minute.
Feeling hot, or increased sweating	Wear a jacket or wrap yourself in blanket in a hot room. Run up and down stairs for five minutes. Do five minutes of moderately intense cardiovascular exercise.
Feeling dizzy	Spin around really fast for one minute. Spin around in a chair for one minute.
Other sensations not listed	How can you creatively conjure up these feelings? (Hint: What activities have you avoided for fear it will bring on these feelings?)

Part B: After you have gotten yourself as anxious as possible (Go, you!), follow these directions:

1. Do ten jumping jacks.

2. Recite the alphabet out loud.

3. Draw a picture of a house.

4. Find five objects with names beginning with the letter T.

5. Count backward from 100 by 7s (100 ... 93 ... and so on).

6. Go to a store and order a drink.

7. Read a news story and then ask yourself, *What is one thing I learned from this article?*

8. Do some more math: what does 856 plus 930 equal?

☞ *Were you able to speak, think, move, communicate with others, and complete multiple commands while experiencing the sensations of anxiety?*

☞ *What do these exercises tell you about your ability to function while on anxiety?*

The key takeaway of this exercise is that it *is* possible to handle complex life tasks when anxious. Would you prefer to not feel anxious while moving through your day and dealing with all the demands of your life? Of course! Anxiety is super uncomfortable. But what's one thing it's not? If you answered "dangerous," you are one step closer to winning the prize of a less anxious brain.

How Is This Exercise Rewiring Your Brain?

When you intentionally bring on the same physical sensations you have when you're anxious, you're teaching your amygdala that it can survive the uncomfortable sensations and is not in danger. With practice, your amygdala will be less reactive to the sensations of anxiety, which will break the anxiety cycle. Your amygdala will learn that it can experience anxiety and still function and perform all required life tasks. You can still move, think, remember, write, and track information when on anxiety.

☞ *On a scale of 1 to 10, rate how much it's a priority for you to continue to work on rewiring your brain to be less reactive and afraid of anxiety.*

KEY TAKEAWAYS

Great work! You've successfully completed your first brain rewiring training session. You've begun training your brain to recognize what anxiety is, and what it isn't. You now understand the function of anxiety and how it's your overeager bodyguard working slightly too hard to keep you safe and sound. You also now understand the biological explanation for all the uncomfortable sensations of anxiety, and you can move forward with this brain rewiring work armed with the critical knowledge that *anxiety may be super uncomfortable, but it's not dangerous*. You're able to acknowledge when anxiety's false alarms are blaring and not let it take you away from doing the things that matter most to you.

CHAPTER 2

Rewire Your Brain to Stop Beating Yourself Up

Zoe and Abby were best friends who did everything together. Upon their return home from their first year of college, they realized they had yet another thing in common: they both had let the fun of college life distract them from healthy living—and they both gained 15 pounds: "the freshman fifteen." They decided to support each other in losing the weight and returning to their more natural body sizes. Together, they would embark on a "summer of health," reining in their out-of-control eating and making exercise a priority.

On Zoe's first day of her summer of health, she snoozed through her alarm several times until she finally forced herself out of bed and realized she now had only twenty minutes to get out of the house to be on time for her summer job. She quickly got dressed and ran out of the house without eating breakfast. After getting settled at her desk, she finally had a moment to pause and realized just how starving she was. She sighed, thinking of the healthy, nutrition-packed smoothie she had planned on making herself for breakfast. For lunch, she was going to pack herself a salad with some leftover grilled chicken from dinner on it. Unfortunately, her morning snoozefest made her dining plans more of a fairy tale than a reality. Instead of her imagined food pyramid–friendly meals, she found herself staring at the office vending machine, deciding between Doritos and Cheetos.

Zoe tried to cheer herself up, reminding herself that even if her nutrition for the day was less than ideal, she could still meet her exercise goals. She imagined that the rest of her workday would be pretty quiet and that she would be able to use her lunch break to take a long walk, get some steps in, and grab something healthy to eat. Instead, she ended up slammed with menial tasks and barely got up from her desk until she left work at six.

After a long day, Zoe found herself sitting on the couch comparing her nutrition and exercise goals for the day with her actual behaviors. It didn't take a fitness guru to realize she had fallen way short of her goals. She was not feeling particularly proud and knew she could do better. She could think of all the excuses in the world to justify why it felt nearly impossible to eat small, healthy meals and exercise the way she had planned, but none of these things mattered. She now realized it was going to be more difficult than she had thought to change her behaviors and prioritize her health. She reflected on what she could have done differently that day, and how to set herself up for a more successful tomorrow. She knew she had it in her to do a better job and reminded herself that to meet her fitness goals, she would have to step up her efforts by being more disciplined.

When Abby woke up on day one of her summer of health, she too had herself a snooze-a-thon until fear took hold and she realized she was going to be late to work. The rest of Abby's day could have been a mirror reflection of Zoe's. She was busy at work from the moment she arrived until the moment she left, and she ate snacks from the vending machine throughout the day when hunger kicked in. When she arrived home after her stressful day, she considered making herself a healthy dinner but instead opted for leftover pizza that was in the refrigerator. After she ate her dinner and finally had a moment to pause and reflect upon her day, she immediately felt sucked into a dark cloud of guilt, regret, and shame. She knew she could still turn things around if she went for a walk or headed to the gym, but instead she sought refuge in her comfy bed. She kept trying to prod herself to get up and accomplish something by pointing out all the ways she was "disgusting" and "a disappointment." With all the insults she hurled at herself, she was no closer to pulling off the covers, throwing on her workout clothes, and heading to the gym. In fact, she felt like the weight of the world was on top of her and she was increasingly hopeless that she would ever be able to create positive change in her life.

Both Zoe and Abby had set similar fitness and nutrition goals for themselves, and they both underperformed based on completing the daily short-term tasks they assigned themselves. They both would need to put more effort into eating healthy and working out in order to meet their goals.

☞ *What is the main difference between how Zoe and Abby handled similar situations of underperforming and failing to meet predefined goals?*

☞ *How do you to tend to handle moments when you feel disappointed in yourself and realize you could have done better? Is it more similar to how Zoe or Abby managed their frustration?*

THE FUNCTION OF ERROR DETECTION

It's important for your brain to recognize when you're acting in a fashion that doesn't promote survival, and based on this assessment, to prompt you to choose a healthier alternative. For example, it wouldn't be helpful for your brain to say, "It's fine that you're sitting around, not working on your project. It'll all work itself out." It's more beneficial for your brain to say, "I know you're tired, and you're warm and cozy watching TV, but you really need to put an hour of work into your project tonight. The term is almost over, and you'll end up causing unnecessary stress." By sending this message, your brain is prompting you to make better choices while also discouraging you from making mistakes that may harm you. It's always slightly uncomfortable to be on the receiving end of your brain's error-detection message, but that mental zap is important to keep you in check and encourage you to make healthier, safer decisions.

When Error Detection Leads to Beating Yourself Up

Your brain's ability to recognize when you're making a potential mistake and to encourage you toward a more adaptive path is critical for survival. You can't live without this brain function. One thing you *can* live without is the self-judgment and shame that often shows up nanoseconds after you receive an error-detection signal. The distinction between the brain sending this signal and the brain getting stuck in shame-and-blame mode can be observed in the difference between how Abby and Zoe handled underperforming at their diet and exercise goals. Zoe's brain observed her shortcomings and sent her the signal: "Mistake. Tomorrow give yourself more time to plan for healthy eating and working out." In contrast, Abby's brain sent this message: "Mistake ... mistake ... mistake. You're hopeless. Just give up because you'll never change."

Zoe's brain followed this path:

Identify mistake → Review what went wrong and what you could do differently → Revise plan

Upon receiving the "mistake" message, Zoe's brain entered problem-solving mode and began identifying barriers to success in order to create a new plan that would increase the likelihood she would meet her diet and exercise goals.

Abby's brain followed this path:

Identify mistake → Review similar past mistakes and their negative consequences → Give up efforts to change; save energy for when you have a chance of winning

For Abby, the "mistake" message initiated a chain of self-critical thoughts that got broader and more generalized until she felt like a complete failure. Once her problems felt that big, it was no longer possible to find a practical solution on how to meet her diet and exercise goals. Over a twenty-four-hour period, Abby's problem shifted from taking in excess calories and not getting enough exercise to "everything you do is wrong." How is Abby's PFC supposed to come up with an effective solution to move past the challenge of that message? When your PFC confronts a problem that is insurmountable, the most reasonable course of action is to admit defeat and save your limited resources for a battle you actually have a chance of winning.

A Fork in the Road

As soon as your brain detects that you have made (or are about to make) a mistake, you'll find yourself at a fork in the road. Your brain can select path A and seamlessly shift from error detection to problem-solving mode. Or it can select path B and seamlessly shift from error detection to beating-yourself-up mode.

Problem-solving mode consists of reviewing what got in the way of meeting your goals, making a plan to avoid these obstacles, and then implementing this revised plan the next time. Beating-yourself-up mode entails simultaneously reviewing all the ways you've messed up in the past, all the ways you'll most likely mess up in the future, and just how unlikely it is that you'll ever be able to effectively tackle the challenge before you.

📖 or 💻
Exercise #5: Where Your Brain Most Often Goes upon Detecting a Mistake

Useful for: Rewiring your brain to just observe and not believe the self-criticism that surfaces when you make an error or underperform.

Time needed: Ten minutes a day

Over the next week, practice noting when you make a mistake or underperform, what thoughts automatically follow, and how you react. Use your journal or download the worksheet (along with a completed sample) at http://www.newharbinger.com/43768 to track key data from these "mistake moments."

☞ *Over the course of the last week, upon making a mistake were you more likely to problem solve or to beat yourself up?*

☞ *Did you notice any shifts in terms of spending less time in beating-yourself-up mode and more time in problem-solving mode as you became a more objective observer of your harsh self-criticism?*

How Is This Exercise Rewiring Your Brain?

The first step in rewiring your brain to spend more time in effective problem solving is to note your go-to patterns of managing "mistake moments." By paying closer attention to your mental chatter, you'll be able to catch yourself more quickly when you're about to beat yourself up, and then override this signal and prompt yourself to choose path A: engaging in effective problem solving. When you activate your PFC, you're telling it what to pay attention to, which will make you more likely to make changes, like ending unhelpful mental habits.

BIOLOGY AND EXPERIENCE INFLUENCE WHICH PATH YOU SELECT

The human brain comes preprogrammed with the ability to offer self-corrections to prevent mistakes, but what you say when you criticize yourself and how often your brain enters beating-yourself-up mode will depend on both your life experiences and your genetics. Some people are naturally more likely to take path A—problem-solving mode—upon receiving an error-detection signal. Others tend to immediately get lured into path B, which eventually leads to the strong belief that error detection and beating yourself up are one and the same.

Your genetics lay the groundwork for how frequently and loudly your inner critic points out your flaws. You may be hardwired to be extremely attuned to what you interpret as mistakes, or you may be programmed to be extremely forgiving of all your shortcomings. You may exist somewhere between these two extremes.

Additionally, the messages you received from your early experiences as a young child also play a role in how quickly and easily you go down the beating-yourself-up path. Overly critical messages from important and close relationships can shape the way you think about yourself. Other difficult life experiences, like trauma or abuse, increase feelings of powerlessness, which then can lead to frequent trips on the self-blame highway, and less practice problem solving your way out of the challenging terrain.

The good news, though, is that even if you have more of a tendency to get stuck in beating-yourself-up mode when you make a mistake (or fear that you might have made one), you can rewire your brain to more frequently and seamlessly enter effective problem-solving mode with targeted exercises and frequent practice.

Rewiring your brain to more readily activate problem-solving mode requires insight, perspective shifting, and flexible thinking— all of which are initiated within your PFC. When you're in tune with your current situation, your PFC can take a step back to see your challenge from a different perspective, opening yourself up to new, innovative ways to move past that challenge.

Research has found that when you think more openly and flexibly, the different areas of your brain are better able to communicate, which can result in more effective problem solving. In fact, research also tells us that when brains are engaged in problem solving, anxious thoughts and feelings typically decrease.

Another area in the middle of your brain, the *striatum*, also helps you engage in problem solving by connecting your desires and intent with your actions. The striatum is guided by reward *and* punishment, both of which motivate you to take (or not take) action. There are three sections of your brain within the striatum, each responsible for different aspects of effective problem solving. One section organizes your thoughts about a problem, another looks at the pros and cons of your options for moving forward, and the third communicates with sensory and motor neurons that link to movement so your body can take action.

You brain in beating-yourself-up mode is operating in the same state of threat detection as it does when experiencing anxiety, although in this case, the threat is from within. Self-criticism signals a threat to your amygdala and leads to a release of all the stress hormones required to battle an enemy.

As you read earlier, the amygdala is designed to quickly detect threats to your safety. When your amygdala feels threatened, it immediately initiates the fight-flight-freeze response. The fight-flight-freeze response increases blood pressure, adrenaline, the hormone cortisol, and all other bodily functions required to mobilize the strength and energy needed to confront or avoid a threat. Although this system was designed by evolution to deal with external attacks, it's just as readily activated by the emotional attacks you make on yourself when you beat yourself up for making a mistake or underperforming.

THE COST OF BEATING YOURSELF UP

Not only is it uncomfortable to have all those stress hormones pulsing through your body, but it's also inefficient and a waste of your limited energy supply.

Imagine the energy a boxer needs to win a fight. Once the match is over, how much energy do you think the boxer has left to accomplish other life tasks that day? By definition, when you use your energy to beat yourself up, you'll have less energy left over to put toward important areas of your life. In addition, you'll have less thinking capacity to focus on getting the job done.

Research tells us that beating yourself up not only consumes your brain's resources but also guides your attention to unhelpful or irrelevant things around you as your brain becomes more reactive to potential threats instead of the current task at hand. Imagine Abby trying to plan her meals for the next day as well as think through realistic options for buying healthy snacks while she's slammed at work and her brain is commenting: "You're a fat, lazy, mess. You're just lying to yourself if you think you're going to eat a protein bar instead of a Snickers. Not only are you pathetic, but you're also delusional." Wouldn't that kind of self-hating rant distract her from accomplishing anything else?

Letting Go of Beating Yourself Up

If we could magically get your brain to stop beating you up, would you take us up on this? The teens we work with are usually quick to say yes; they describe how bad it feels to be on the receiving end of all this self-criticism, and how desperately they want to eliminate this ineffective thinking style. But when we talk further, they often become hesitant. They begin to recognize their fears around letting go of self-criticism. They often bring up concerns about becoming too complacent and lazy, and they're not sure how else they will create change if they stop beating themselves up.

These common misconceptions are associated with beating yourself up: beating myself up (1) encourages effective action, (2) keeps me from being complacent and accepting the status quo, (3) is a deserved punishment for my past mistakes, and (4) reminds me of my mistakes so that I can avoid making the same ones again.

But in reality, beating yourself up will only keep you hostage to shame, fear, and anxiety. What *will* help you move forward and engage in effective problem solving is becoming a positive coach for yourself.

Exercise #6: From Automatic Shame to Understanding

Useful for: Rewiring your brain to shift from its automatic self-criticism to a more kind and understanding stance when thinking about past mistakes.

Time needed: Five minutes

Close your eyes, and imagine the last big mistake you made. Open your eyes. What did your brain immediately tell you about yourself? Jot this down in your journal.

Next, try adopting a kinder, more forgiving, and understanding voice in response to this memory. Jot this new response down.

☞ *Did the anxiety in your body feel any different?*

Positive vs. Punitive Coaching from an External Source

Ethan was having a rough tennis practice. He had had a hard time sleeping the night before because he was worried about his finals. He told himself he would just do his best at practice and hoped his performance would not be impacted by his less-than-ideal mental state. Ethan's coach, Fernando, immediately laid into him. He asked if there was something wrong with Ethan and questioned his commitment to the sport. He said he had other kids he could be coaching who would not be wasting his time. He ended his rant by informing Ethan that with his attitude he would not amount to anything.

Exercise #7: Good Coach vs. Bad Coach

Useful for: Rewiring a brain that needs help noticing when its punitive coach is in charge of training.

Time needed: Twenty minutes

Part A: Use your journal to write down your answers to these questions.

- How do you think Ethan is feeling as his coach berates him?

- How motivated do you think Ethan is to do a good job?

- How confident do you think Ethan is feeling?

- How strong and capable do you think Ethan is feeling?

- How likely do you think it is that Ethan will play well the next time he has a training session with Coach Fernando?

Think of a time in your own life when someone coached you in a harsh, aggressive fashion.

- How did it make you feel?

- How motivated for success were you after this interaction?

Now, think of a time when someone coached you in an encouraging, supportive manner.

- How did it make you feel?

- How motivated for success were you after this interaction?

Part B: You'll need your phone or a recording device for this experiment to assess how beating yourself up impacts your performance.

First, make an audio file with your top beating-yourself-up thoughts. For example, Abby recorded herself saying, "You're a loser. A pathetic, lazy loser." Next, try completing a few tasks that require focus and attention, such as building a house out of cards, walking with a book on your head, or doing homework.

Next, make an audio file with positive coaching content on it. Abby recorded this message: "Just because you're struggling in one area doesn't erase all your other successes. You can meet your weight-loss goals if you just focus on taking baby steps." Next, try completing the same tasks you selected above.

Compare and contrast your performance. Did you notice any differences between how long it took you to complete tasks, how many errors you made, and how often your attention drifted from the task at hand when you were receiving harsh self-criticism versus positive coaching?

Part C: Go through one whole day focusing on all the things you have done wrong, are currently doing wrong, and will likely do wrong in the future. The following day, work on noticing whenever your brain gets stuck in beating-yourself-up mode, and when you catch yourself, tell yourself, *For today I choose to accept myself with all my strengths and weaknesses.*

Compare and contrast the days. How much did you accomplish? How was your overall mood? How much energy did you have? How motivated did you feel to engage in your life? Which kind of reaction would you like more of?

How Is This Exercise Rewiring Your Brain?

For any athlete, having a positive, supportive coach helps enhance performance and increase the likelihood of winning. Your brain deserves a positive coach, not a punitive one. By rewiring your brain to serve as a positive coach, you're freeing up your PFC so it can use its resources to focus, learn, and engage in problem solving when confronted with an obstacle. When your internal punitive coach is running the show, you'll feel more fear, anxiety, and panic, making it more difficult for you to create positive change in your life.

Common "Beating-Yourself-Up" Issues Specific to Those Struggling with Anxiety

It's likely that after many years of struggling with an anxious brain, you've begun to judge yourself in negative terms. Struggling with anxiety has a way of making you feel broken or flawed or weak or … (*insert your own go-to self-judgment*). It's easy to get stuck in the "shame-and-blame" game about struggling with anxiety, and never get to actually working on it. Of course, as you've already read, beating yourself up about struggling with anxiety, or anything else, really does nothing to help you move forward. In fact, it keeps you trapped. Which is more helpful: spending hours yelling at yourself for being overweight, or one hour going to the gym and getting closer to your health and fitness goals? We would rather you use your energy toward meeting your behavioral health goal than further imprisoning yourself in anxiety, shame, and anger.

These are the judgments we most often hear teens make about themselves due to their struggles with anxiety:

- You're a loser.

- You're pathetic.

- You're disgusting.

- You're weak.

- You're defective.

☞ *What are your go-to judgments?*

Pain of Anxiety vs. Suffering Due to Anxiety

Imagine you're experiencing an uncomfortable anxiety symptom and are receiving a strong (yet inaccurate) signal that you're in danger. You begin yelling at yourself, "You're such a loser. What's wrong with you?" Will this likely (1) lead to your anxious moment passing more quickly, (2) lead to your anxious moment lasting longer, or (3) have no impact on your anxiety?

If you answered (2), you're correct. Yelling at yourself to be strong will only make you feel more distress, which will prolong your anxiety. It's time to practice serving as a positive self-coach.

📖 or 💻
Exercise #8: Positive Coaching Slogans

Useful for: Rewiring a brain to know what to do when anxious thoughts and self-criticism set in.

Time needed: Fifteen minutes

Write down as many positive coaching slogans as you can think of for future moments of anxiety. What is key is that they must be authentic. If you tell yourself, "You're strong and brave" but don't believe it, it won't do any good. Here are a few slogans teens we work with have used:

- I've survived all the difficult moments in my past.

- Anxiety does not define me.

- It might not be okay now, but it'll be okay soon enough.

- Anxiety is not me; anxiety is moving through me.

- I'm stronger than anxiety.

- Just one step at a time.

For the next week, write down each anxious moment you experience, and rate your initial level of anxiety on a scale of 1 to 10. Next, note your automatic self-critical thoughts. Remind yourself of your positive coaching slogans, and then note your new anxiety level. You can use your journal or the worksheet you can download at http://www.newharbinger.com/43768, where you'll also see a sample entry. To get the most out of this brain rewiring training plan, it's critical to work on letting go of self-criticism and to conserve your energy for the hard work of facing your fears.

What Would You Tell a Good Friend?

Disengaging from beating-yourself-up mode is unfortunately more complicated than simply telling yourself to stop. It's often easier to imagine a kind response you would offer a good friend than it is to imagine offering the same TLC to yourself. So let's consider how you might help a friend who is feeling stressed and anxious about their future and unsure if they're making the right choices to set themself up for a successful life. Which response would be helpful?

- Get over it, you big baby.

- Learn to deal.

- What's wrong with you?

- That's hard but it's normal to feel scared and unsure about the future. I believe in your ability to figure it all out.

It's amazingly healing when someone acknowledges your pain with a simple "Yeah, that *is* hard," instead of ignoring it or telling you to suck it up. Recognizing that something is uncomfortable is not an excuse for behaving badly, but it's an effective first step in deciding how to proceed despite the pain.

How Is This Exercise Rewiring Your Brain?

When you positively coach yourself through a challenging moment instead of solely relying on your harsh inner critic, your cortisol levels (stress hormones) decrease. Your body starts to signal your brain that you no longer need to panic or engage in fight-flight-freeze mode; the internal threat is no longer so threatening. You feel safer, which then allows your brain to be more open and less stuck in frustration. Another hormone, oxytocin, increases when you engage in positive self-coaching. Oxytocin makes you feel cared for and connected to yourself and to others and elicits that warm, fuzzy feeling you get when someone does something kind for you. We know from research that the more frequently people engage in positive coaching (instead of self-criticism), the less anxious and depressed they typically feel. By rewiring your brain to offer positive coaching, you'll feel less shame and be better able to focus on the important things in your life.

KEY TAKEAWAYS

By offering yourself a "Yeah, that *is* hard *and* I believe you're strong enough to get through it" rather than shaming and blaming and judging yourself for struggling, you're both acknowledging the discomfort and reminding your brain that you can push through the struggle.

Moving forward, when you notice you're feeling anxious yet aren't in a truly dangerous situation, practice positively coaching yourself through the false alarm with patience and compassion. Try to offer yourself the same kindness you would offer to a friend who was struggling with an anxious moment.

CHAPTER 3

Rewire Your Brain to Be Here Now

School ended for the day, and Dan and Kelly exited the building, heading opposite ways toward their homes. As Dan walked along the street, his mind pinged between anxious thoughts about an upcoming calculus quiz, worry about how he's been performing on the basketball team, and frustration that some of his friends have been taking more jabs at him than usual when they "joke" around. Dan got so lost in his own thoughts that he barely noticed his walk home and was surprised to suddenly be at his front door. His stomach was tied in knots, and his mind continued to dart between upsetting thoughts as he walked into his house.

Kelly, meanwhile, was centered and calm as she took her walk. Stressful thoughts occasionally entered her mind, but she simply noticed them, then returned to her present experience. When the worry came into her mind, *What if I get a bad score on my calculus quiz and can't get into my dream college?* she focused instead on the cool fall air against her skin and the crunch of leaves under her feet. She felt a strong sense of contentment and was refreshed and focused as she walked through her front door. Kelly knew she couldn't do anything about her calculus quiz while she was walking down the sidewalk anyway; she realized that getting swept up in worry would just make her feel worse now and make it harder to concentrate later, when it was finally time to study.

Once settled in their homes for the evening, both Dan and Kelly prepared to study for tomorrow's calculus quiz. Dan's stomach was still in knots, and his mind was completely unfocused. Every time he opened his calculus book, his attention was flooded with more worries about the exam, leading to worries about college, leading to worries about future jobs and even retirement. His heart was pounding. He felt like his mind was a wild horse running in any direction it wanted. To get some relief, he turned on his PlayStation and zoned out to the comfort of video games. All the while, however, a sinking feeling about the quiz was growing in his stomach. It got harder and harder to put down the remote and open his book. He finally managed to study around midnight, but he was so anxious that none of the material made any sense. He took the quiz the next day and was able to answer only about half the questions.

Kelly, on the other hand, was feeling relaxed and focused as she prepared to study. Her walk home was invigorating, a nice break from school. She felt grounded and calm as she opened her calculus book. Some anxious thoughts came into her mind, but rather than getting swept away by them, she simply told herself, *There's an anxious thought*, then returned to focusing on her work; it was almost like saying, "There's my dog on the couch" or "There's a banana on the counter." She didn't get lost in analyzing *why* the dog was on the couch or the banana was on the counter or the anxious thought was in her head. She just noticed the thought, then returned to the present moment—in this case, her studies. She took the quiz the next day and got a higher score than she had predicted.

What's the moral of this story? In part, it's that Kelly is more *mindful* than Dan. She's better at staying grounded in the present moment, rather than getting swept away in thoughts about other people, places, and times. As a result, she tends to feel more relaxed and happy, have better concentration, and even be in better physical health than Dan. But the moral doesn't stop there. Even more importantly, Kelly actively trains her brain to be mindful through daily exercises that you'll soon read about.

MINDFULNESS AND THE BRAIN

You've probably heard the term "mindfulness" thrown around before—it's certainly trendy these days! But mindfulness meditation is actually rooted in ancient Buddhist practices that date back over thirty-five hundred years. What exactly is mindfulness? It's often defined as nonjudgmental focus on present-moment experience. And what is mindfulness meditation? It involves different methods for rewiring your brain to be more mindful.

Let's unpack all that for a moment. Notice that nowhere in the definition of "mindfulness" or "meditation" does it say anything about turning off your thoughts, or blocking negative ones, or not getting distracted. Far from it! Mindfulness is all about noticing the full range of your present-moment experience, without negatively reacting to or trying to change it. When you meditate, as you'll soon learn, you may be shocked to see all the places your mind goes, bouncing here and there and all over. Again, the goal is never to block or turn off your thoughts. Instead, it's simply to notice them, like Kelly did, and then return to the present moment again and again. Through this practice, you'll find you become more centered and less anxious, feeling more confident and grounded in your life.

Although mindfulness practice may seem simple, it's also incredibly powerful. Thanks to neuroimaging studies of the brain, we now know that the benefits of regular meditation practice may include your amygdala decreasing in size and becoming less activated; your PFC going offline and taking a break from worrying and creating escape plans; your hippocampus increasing in size, which helps with memory and learning; and decreased aging in your brain. Meditation also appears to change the size of other brain areas to increase empathy and compassion, and decrease unrealistic or unhelpful thoughts about yourself. And these changes, in turn, can have a profound impact on your daily life. People who regularly meditate show decreases in anxiety, stress, and depression; greater feelings of happiness and satisfaction with their relationships; better sleep quality; and even better immune functioning and fewer sick days. That's pretty incredible!

Exercise #9: Set Up Your Own Mindfulness Meditation Practice

Useful for: Rewiring a brain that needs some extra help staying in the present moment.

Time needed: About ten minutes

This first exercise will help you establish your personal mindfulness meditation practice. You'll need your cell phone or some other device with an Internet connection.

We suggest trying to meditate for about ten minutes each day, but evidence shows that doing more is even better for your health, and doing less can still be very helpful. It doesn't matter if you do it in the morning, evening, or a different time each day, although setting a regular schedule seems to help some people.

To start out, you'll want to find a space where you won't be interrupted by anyone else. If possible, find somewhere you don't use for other things. This doesn't have to be a whole room, or anything big like that. Most people have great success picking a small corner of their bedroom that they don't usually sit in, or maybe sitting in front of the window in their room and looking out at a tree. The basic idea is that you're setting up a special area that is just for you to practice meditation. It's a good idea to grab a cushion to sit on (or a chair, if it makes you more comfortable), and set something in your line of sight that you find soothing to look at—maybe a stone you picked up on a hike, or a statue or candle you like. If you share a room, you could pack these things up when you're done meditating, then take them back out for your next session. Your meditation space should be simple but cozy, all your own.

Next, you'll want to turn on a guided meditation practice. You can meditate without one, but most people find it easier to do with a guide. Plus, if you're new to meditation, the guide will help instruct you in what to do. There are tons of different options for guided meditations. Some have you meditate with your eyes open, and others with your eyes closed. Some give special guidance for calming your mind in different settings, like when on a train or going into a meeting, and others give more general advice. We encourage you to explore different options by typing "meditation" into the app store, and finding a meditation app that feels like a good fit for you. If you don't have a phone or computer, you can also borrow guided meditations from almost any local library.

If you want to start meditating without a guide, you can do so by following these simple instructions. First, set your soothing object within view and take a seat in your meditation spot. You can sit on a chair with your feet flat on the ground, or cross-legged on a pillow. The important thing is that your spine is straight and that you aren't lying down. If you are, you're likely to fall asleep.

Once you're seated, gently rest your gaze on your object. You might part your lips slightly, letting air flow smoothly in and out. Try to bring a completely nonjudgmental awareness to the object, perhaps viewing it as though you're an alien from another planet who has never seen such a thing before and therefore doesn't have all sorts of stories about it. Simply notice its shape and its colors, its shadows and angles. Whenever you start to have judgments or thoughts, getting lost in stories about the object or your own past or future, just notice where your mind has gone, and then bring it back to noticing the qualities of your object. Remember, you're not trying to block out thoughts; you're simply learning to notice where your mind goes, and not to get carried away by distractions. You're observing your own thoughts, without judgment, and then learning to come back to the present moment.

A word to the wise: When you meditate, whether it's with a guided recording or our instructions, you'll have all sorts of experiences. Some days your thoughts will seem like a storm, nearly unending and impossible to get out from under. Other days your thoughts and feelings will seem more like clouds that float by peacefully. Truly, there is no "right" or "wrong" experience. Everyone has stormy practices and calm practices. Just by showing up to your spot and practicing returning to the present moment—no matter how drenched in "rain" (distracting thoughts) you may feel—you are rewiring your brain and bringing about the tremendous benefits so many people before you have gained from meditation. In fact, it may be your very "stormiest" days that ultimately bring the greatest rewiring benefits!

How Is This Exercise Rewiring Your Brain?

When you engage in your personalized meditation practice, you're rewiring your brain to not instantly react to the "alarm bells" that cause anxiety by weakening the association between your bodily sensations (fight-flight-freeze cues) and thoughts about yourself or things around you. Remember, your amygdala may even shrink and be less active as a result of meditation, leading to fewer false alarms. Meditation has also been linked to increased amounts of *gray matter* (the areas of the brain that have many, many neurons) in your hippocampus and PFC, which can lead to more feelings of positivity, emotional stability, and improved concentration. Increased serotonin and oxytocin lead to improvements in your mood, while better focus happens with more of the chemical called dopamine, all as a result of meditation practice. Meditation also helps with lowering the stress hormones cortisol and adrenaline, the ones that increase during fight-flight-freeze mode. It even helps you sleep by increasing your melatonin hormones, which controls your wake-sleep cycle.

☞ *On a scale of 1 to 10, rate how much it's a priority for you to continue to work on establishing your own personal meditation practice.*

Exercise #10: 3-3-3 Tool for Staying Grounded in Daily Life

Useful for: Rewiring a brain that feels super ungrounded when you're going about your day.

Time needed: About three minutes

How can you incorporate mindfulness into your daily life off the meditation cushion, especially when you're feeling most "ungrounded"? Feeling ungrounded means different things for different people—maybe your mind races, maybe your heart starts to pound, maybe you feel disconnected from your own body, almost as though you're watching it from above. Maybe you just feel super stressed, like you're about to freak out. Whatever the symptoms, the 3-3-3 exercise is a simple but powerful tool that has helped many people quickly calm their minds and return to the present moment.

You can do this exercise anywhere and don't need any supplies. To start, sit up straight with your feet flat on the ground and your hands resting on your thighs. The key is for your spine to be straight, like a stack of coins, and the rest of your body to be loose and relaxed, almost draped on your straight spine. Take a moment to settle yourself in this posture.

Then, look around the space you're in, and name three things you see; for example, *Right now I see my dog, a book, and a plant.* Try not to get into judging the things you see in any way. For instance, you'd want to simply say "book" to yourself, rather than getting into a whole mental story like, *My mom gave it to me, and I never read it because I doubt it's any good but I still feel bad I haven't read it.*

The goal here is to be in the present, not getting caught up in judgments or concepts. Many of the teens we work with find it especially calming to notice a spot where the wall meets the floor of the room they're in. There's something grounding about it, especially if you're feeling disconnected from your body or anxious within it. So one of the things you notice might be that spot.

Next, name three things you feel. These are physical sensations rather than emotions; for example, *I feel the sleeve of my sweater on my arm, the hard floor under my feet, and the smooth metal of my necklace against my skin.*

Finally, name three things you hear: *Right now, I hear my dog's collar jingling as she scratches her ear, the sound of the air moving through the vents, and a car driving by outside.* This one might take you a moment.

Now that you have the basic idea, try the whole 3-3-3 exercise for yourself from the top: Sit up straight, with your body relaxed and grounded. Slow down for a moment, and say three things you see, three things you feel, and three things you hear. You can say the things out loud, or if you're in a public space, you can just say them in your head. You can repeat this exercise as many times as you need, although people often find that doing it even once calms them down a great deal.

How Is This Exercise Rewiring Your Brain?

Part of the reason this exercise is so powerful is that it grounds you in your physical senses. When you're grounded, it allows your brain to focus on what is happening in the present moment, and not get so caught up in a worry spiral that goes on in your PFC. With practice, the 3-3-3 mindfulness exercise helps rewire your PFC to take a break from planning, worrying, and imagining frightening outcomes. You rewire your PFC to focus on what is directly in front of it: what you see, feel, and hear. Because the mindfulness exercise also helps disengage unrealistic thoughts about yourself, you're rewiring your brain to simply notice your bodily sensations and the world around you as it all is, without linking it to fear or danger.

☞ *On a scale of 1 to 10, rate how much it's a priority for you to continue using the 3-3-3 tool to rewire your brain to get grounded in daily life.*

KEY TAKEAWAYS

Mindfulness is nonjudgmental awareness of your current experience. It does not mean turning off your thoughts, but rather becoming less reactive to them, which in turn helps you stay grounded in the present. Rewiring your brain to be more mindful—for example, through ten minutes of daily meditation practice and using the 3-3-3 tool—can dramatically improve your mental and physical health.

CHAPTER 4

Rewire Your Brain to Move Past Emotional Pain

It's Friday evening, and Carly and Ella were both taking showers as they got ready to go out. Both nicked their legs while shaving, drawing blood. "Ouch!" Carly exclaimed, as a sharp feeling of pain ran across her leg. Within a moment the pain stopped, and Carly continued showering, enjoying the warm water against her back and thinking with excitement about the party she was going to. When she got out of the shower, she stuck a Band-Aid on her leg and continued getting ready, not giving the cut a second thought.

Ella also called out "Ouch!" when she cut herself, but her reactions didn't stop there. *I'm so clumsy!* Ella thought. *I always do this. I'm such an idiot. Now I can't wear a skirt, and my whole outfit is ruined. Why do I always mess things up?* As she got out of the shower and put on a Band-Aid, Ella got even more negative. *Now I've got a giant symbol on my leg of what an idiot I am,* she thought. That night, each time she thought about nicking herself, she became frustrated at herself all over again.

What's the moral of this story? It's that Carly is less *reactive* to negative events. Please note we didn't say the moral is that Carly never reacts negatively to anything at all. If you cut yourself, you'll feel pain. It's just human nature. Yelling "Ouch!" is what we call a *pain response*—your immediate, almost unavoidable response to something challenging. It's how you *react* to the pain that can get you into trouble, particularly if you have a catastrophic reaction where you really blow things out of proportion. In addition to having a pain response, Ella reacts by launching into a whole self-critical rant. Long after the immediate physical pain of cutting her skin, Ella is still creating all sorts of emotional distress by diving into a story about what the cut meant: that she's clumsy, screws everything up, and on and on. Pain responses are unavoidable; having them is part of what it means to be alive. Catastrophic pain reactions are generally not necessary, and just make us feel worse. Thinking about anxious suffering, we can break this down as follows:

Suffering = Built-in pain of a challenge + Catastrophic reaction to the challenge

Can you think of times when you got lost in catastrophic reactions to a legitimately difficult event, and it led to way more suffering than was necessary? Maybe you got a bad score on a test, then got lost in endless thoughts about how you'd never get into your dream college. Or you said something "dumb," then beat yourself up for weeks, or played poorly in a game and convinced yourself your teammates would hold it against you for the rest of the season. Luckily, through mindfulness practice, we can learn to see painful experiences for what they are, and pull ourselves out of catastrophe land, becoming less and less unnecessarily reactive to the negative things that happen in our lives.

PAIN, REACTIVITY, AND THE BRAIN

As you've probably figured out by this point in the book (not to mention just by being alive), life is full of hard moments. It's normal—and in fact very healthy—to experience negative feelings when we face tough times. Just as you get wet when you go swimming, you likely feel anxious or hurt when friends exclude you. This immediate feeling of discomfort is your pain reaction. It doesn't mean anything about you other than that you're confronting a tough time. When you're mindful during hard experiences—simply experiencing whatever comes up without jumping to the future or getting stuck in the past—your brain is actually in a very good place.

There is a reason your brain feels pain, whether the source is physical or emotional. Your brain is alerting you to something important. It signals that your body or mind needs protection. Think about the pain you feel if you accidentally touch a pan of fresh-baked cookies right from the oven. You sense intense heat on your fingers, which then sends this message through specific sensory neurons that are responsible for communicating "This is painful!" to different areas of your brain. Then your brain helps protect you from further damage by activating a useful withdrawal reflex. Your hippocampus uses its learning and memory resources to signal that it's now time to treat your burn, so you rush to the sink and hold your hand under cool water. Your brain also releases pain-fighting hormones called endorphins. So while you first felt a sharp pain when you burned your hand, that pain soon turns into a dull ache. The intensity, although still painful, weakens over time. When you're mindful of your pain (however uncomfortable it may be), you can be better tuned into what your body needs to help relieve and protect yourself from further pain.

Where you get into trouble is when you're no longer mindful, and instead get lost in reactions. You take a single event—like cutting your leg or getting a bad test score—and spin way off in your own mind, catastrophizing and telling yourself elaborate stories about what these things mean about you and the future. When these reactions happen, your mind and body suffer. In fact, they will likely lead you to feel worse than the initial pain caused by that single event. Research suggests that catastrophizing leads you to focus even more on your painful experience, making it hard to recognize other indications that your pain is actually subsiding. As you continue to focus on how bad the pain feels, you start to interpret this discomfort as threatening, leading to intense emotions. When you're stuck in catastrophic reactions, your PFC is activated as it prepares you for all the worst possible outcomes. Your PFC tells you that bad test score means that you are, and always will be, a failure. And how are you supposed to live your life as a complete failure? Well, that scary thought alerts your amygdala to fear and panic, activating your fight-flight-freeze response, and prolonging the anxiety for long after you've received your test score. Luckily, there are ways to rewire your brain to be more mindful during hard times, reducing your reactions and becoming less anxious.

Exercise #11: Notice and Come Out of Catastrophic Reactions

Useful for: Rewiring a brain that is highly reactive to negative events.

Time needed: One day

For the next day, try to notice every time you experience a catastrophic reaction. This could range from major reactions, like assuming that because you got a bad score on a test you'll never go to a good college and have the career you want, to more minor reactions like telling yourself you're an "idiot" because of something embarrassing you said. If you have trouble remembering to do this, you could put up a sticky note on your bedroom door or in a book you use regularly at school that simply says "Reactions." Negative feelings can be another very good reminder. Each time you're feeling unhappy, use that negative emotion as a reminder to stop and check if you're experiencing any catastrophic reactions.

If you're experiencing a catastrophic reaction, it's a good time to pull your mind out of its judgmental, catastrophizing spiral, and come back to the present moment. The 3-3-3 exercise is a great method for doing this. Remember: pause, straighten your spine, then name three things you see, three things you feel, and three things you hear. Once you've interrupted your catastrophic reaction even a little, go on to focusing on something in your present life, like petting your dog, finishing your homework, or cooking some food. If catastrophic reactions start to strike again, simply notice them, and practice coming back to the present again. The more you do this, the fewer and further between your catastrophic reactions will become. And remember, it's like going to the gym: Working out once won't suddenly mean you're in good shape forever, and it might even feel hard and frustrating the first times. But the more you work out, the stronger and healthier you become.

How Is This Exercise Rewiring Your Brain?

When you get caught in the pain and discomfort of catastrophic reactions, your PFC likes to conjure up the worst-case scenarios and scare your amygdala into thinking it needs to take action (about things that haven't even happened!). Instead, when you notice this happening, you're giving your PFC a reality check and reminding it that you don't need to think beyond the initial discomfort. You remind your PFC that the discomfort is giving you some information to alert your body or mind to take some type of action. This action does not have to be the immediate, your-life-is-in-danger, fight-flight-freeze type. When you practice just sitting with the discomfort, your brain has the opportunity to learn, like for all emotions, that the discomfort will pass. And through research, we know that people who meditate have better control of where their attention goes, so they are less consumed by the unhelpful thoughts and can shift to some more helpful ones in the present moment. The more you practice noticing your catastrophic reactions and refocusing on your immediate experience, the easier it will be for your brain to readjust during especially painful times. Your brain rewires your ability to shift from reacting based on emotion to being mindful of what you feel in the present moment.

☞ *On a scale of 1 to 10, rate how much it's a priority for you to continue to work on noticing and interrupting your catastrophic reactions.*

Exercise #12: Take Away the Power from Catastrophic Reactions

Useful for: Rewiring a brain that gets stuck in catastrophizing.

Time needed: Five to ten minutes

Sometimes, as hard as you try, you'll find you just can't pull yourself out of a catastrophic reaction. In these cases, the best approach may be to actually meditate on your own catastrophic thoughts and feelings, simply observing the reaction itself without judgment.

Take a seat in your meditation posture, and invite the catastrophic reaction to join you. When it marches in—and we're sure it'll be happy to do so—imagine you're watching the reaction occurring in a character on TV or in a movie, rather than experiencing it yourself. This creates a little distance, letting you be more objective. You might even imagine you're a scientist who is interested in noticing every detail about the catastrophic thoughts but doesn't get caught up in them. Go ahead and describe to yourself out loud everything you notice about the reaction, being as objective as you can. For example, you might say, "This catastrophic reaction is causing the thought *Because I said one embarrassing thing to Amy, she's not going to want to continue hanging out, and soon I won't have any friends at all*. Now that thought is making my heart beat faster and my chest feel tight."

An important thing to recognize during this exercise is that you *will* experience pain reactions during it—and that's completely okay. In the example above, having a thought about not having any friends caused the immediate "pain" reaction of the heart beating faster and the chest getting tight. This is normal. Even having more catastrophic thoughts is okay. The goal is simply to avoid becoming so swept up in the catastrophic reaction that you forget your reaction is not reality. It's the difference between remembering you're watching a movie, even if it scares you, and being so absorbed in the plot that you forget that the movie isn't your real life.

Continue with this process of nonjudgmentally observing your catastrophic experience. You'll find that it becomes quite empowering to be able to watch your reactions without getting swept away by them. Just as if you watch a movie enough times you'll come to know how each scene goes, eventually you'll know by heart the "plot" of your catastrophic reactions. It won't surprise you when certain thoughts come up, causing your body to respond in certain ways. Instead, you'll be able to simply observe the catastrophic reaction as it happens, maybe even getting a bit bored of it, and then return to the rest of your life.

How Is This Exercise Rewiring Your Brain?

As you've probably noticed, those catastrophic reactions can bring up unpleasant and unhelpful thoughts that keep you stuck feeling uncomfortable. This exercise helps you use mindfulness techniques that let these thoughts move on from your brain. When you're engaged in mindfulness meditation, it can help deactivate the area within the PFC that is responsible for all the unhelpful chatter in your brain. Meditation practice can also help make these negative thoughts feel less intrusive, making fewer surprise appearances in your brain. Practice with mindfully noticing your catastrophic thoughts makes it easier to see a thought as just a thought, instead of judging it or making meaning of each one. With less meaning attached to your thoughts, your amygdala learns to not instantly react to what are simply words within a thought. And your PFC learns to respond in a different way. It learns that it does not need to keep churning out mental chatter and frightening what-if images. Through consistent meditation (or nonjudgmental observation of your catastrophic reaction), your brain rewires itself to shrink your amygdala so that it does not instantly react with fight-flight-freeze mode when negative thoughts pop up.

☞ *On a scale of 1 to 10, rate how much it's a priority for you to continue to work on rewiring your brain to take the power from catastrophic reactions.*

KEY TAKEAWAYS

Pain responses are your immediate reactions to unpleasant events, like feeling physical pain if you cut your skin. They are a fact of life, like getting wet if you go in water. Catastrophic reactions are all the negative stories and judgments you have about your negative experiences, which just make you feel worse. Through mindfulness, you can become less reactive to negative experiences, feeling more grounded and less anxious.

CHAPTER 5

Rewire Your Brain to Be Resilient

Dave was passionate about tennis. He loved the game and constantly sought opportunities to progress. He always asked his coach for tips on what he could do to improve, and he looked for extra practice time. His coach told him there was a new group forming that he might qualify for, but the majority of players were at a slightly higher level; he would have to "check his ego at the door" and tolerate frequent losses. Dave took some time to consider this opportunity. He had to be honest with himself about how uncomfortable it made him to lose, and how easily he could psych himself out when he felt lacking in any way. At the same time, his love of the game and desire to grow as a player were undeniable. He felt torn and decided to give himself a couple of days to consider the pros and cons of participating in this more advanced group. After deliberating for what felt like an eternity, Dave realized he was never going to feel ready to risk feeling bad about himself and less-than in comparison to the other players, but that didn't mean it was not the right thing to do. He decided that tolerating the uncomfortable thoughts and feelings he knew would inevitably show up was worth it in order to get to the next level and put himself in a position to achieve his goals.

Caleb was also passionate about tennis. Since he was a young kid, he had been dedicating a lot of time and energy to the sport. In addition to all the training and lessons Caleb had over the years, he was also a natural athlete and quickly picked up new skills and techniques. Tennis, as well as many other aspects of life, came easy to him, and he rarely had to struggle to achieve or progress. But lately, something was happening with Caleb's tennis game; he just felt out of sync, as though he had hit a wall of some sort and couldn't find his game. He spoke with his coach about his recent underwhelming performance. His coach suggested that he play with the same group Dave was considering; he needed to be playing in a more competitive, challenging environment to continue to improve. His coach gave him the same warning he had given Dave—that he would be competing against a higher caliber of players and had to be prepared to lose at the beginning. Caleb said he would think this over and get back to him. Caleb spent hours imagining what it would be like to lose and exist at the bottom of the pack. He thought about how embarrassed and angry he would feel having to face these other players, knowing he would likely be one of the weaker players. As worries and uncertainty took hold, he started having problems falling asleep at night. The daytime hours were not much better, as his brain raced and reviewed the same fears over and over again. After a week of what felt like endless torture, he told his coach he was going to pass on the opportunity and continue to play with his current team. He felt immediate relief, like a thousand-ton brick had been lifted off his chest. But this comfort did not last long. After a day or so, he began to regret his decision. He couldn't stop thinking about the missed opportunity, yet at the same time, he couldn't imagine surviving the feelings of failure that would come along with taking the next step. He felt stuck and hopeless, and could not think his way out of his predicament.

When considering your own ability to handle life's frustrating moments, do you relate more to how Dave or Caleb handled their tennis-team dilemmas? One way to think through this question is to review a challenging moment you've experienced over the past few weeks and assess how much distress and discomfort it caused you.

☞ Think of one frustrating moment you recently experienced. What were you doing? Who were you with? When did it occur?

☞ Describe how you felt when confronted by this difficult situation.

☞ Rate your peak distress level at the most frustrating point of this experience, on a scale from 1 to 10.

☞ What is your best guess as to how the average person would handle the situation you just described? Try asking a few friends or family members how much distress they imagine they would experience if the same situation happened to them. Did you experience more or less emotional distress than they predicted for themselves?

As you're no doubt well aware, life comes jam-packed with hard moments. There's no way around this truth. You can try to make good decisions, work hard, and do the right thing, yet there will always be bumps in the road that must be navigated. So while we can't offer you a magic solution to completely eradicate life's difficult moments, we can help you experience less emotional suffering when confronted by these inevitable challenges.

As you read in the previous chapter, emotional suffering is not just made up of the direct pain a challenging situation brings. Emotional suffering consists of both the pain built into a difficult situation, and your emotional reaction to the situation. For example, if you stub your toe, you'll inevitably experience a level of pain that seems shockingly intense given how tiny that toe is.

But if you were to yell at yourself and tell yourself you should have been more careful, or if you stomp your feet in frustration, or worse, punch yourself in the arm because you're so annoyed at yourself, you'll feel more overall emotional suffering than if you (1) notice the excruciating momentary pain, (2) remind yourself to slow down a bit, and (3) proceed with your day and pay better attention to your environment moving forward.

In the previous chapter, you learned how mindfulness can help you disentangle pain from suffering, and even reduce the suffering you feel. In doing so, mindfulness helps your brain become more *resilient*. Resiliency is a super important tool that provides you with the ability to move past hardship, as opposed to getting thrown off course when life offers you a heaping serving of discomfort. When you engage your "resiliency muscles," you're able to bounce back rather than getting bent out of shape when confronted by a challenging situation. Rewiring your brain to enhance these abilities will help you successfully face discomfort and in doing so reduce your overall emotional suffering. Resiliency doesn't mean you enjoy or seek out difficulty. But it does mean that when it inevitably surfaces, you have confidence in your ability to manage, cope, and survive.

RESILIENCY AND THE BRAIN

Your brain is wired to reward you for seeking out situations that make you feel good and safe. Similarly, your brain sends you signals to encourage you to avoid situations that are uncomfortable and potentially dangerous. The memories of both positive and negative situations are processed in an area of the brain called the *nucleus accumbens*, where dopamine is released. Dopamine plays a role in many of our brain functions, including sleep, movement, motivation, reward, memory, arousal, and attention. When faced with a poten-tial distressing situation, dopamine anticipates what might make you feel good or not so good, and motivates you to act accordingly. It reminds you of how rewarding or uncomfortable similar moments were in the past and encourages you to move toward pleasure over pain in the moment and the future.

When you're in an uncomfortable situation and choose to retreat, dopamine floods your brain. Your brain is rewarding you for your escape act with a heaping serving of this feel-good chemical. If the signal from your nucleus accumbens came with words, it would sound something like this: "Go, you! You just escaped a saber-toothed tiger! You deserve a special reward for keeping us alive and fleeing so swiftly from that dangerous situation. I'm going to gift you with a big, juicy serving of dopamine. And now you'll be all the more likely to remember the next time you face this situation that it's super important to flee for your life. Enjoy!"

So far, all this sounds pretty fair and effective. What could pos-sibly be the downside of your brain rewarding you with dopamine when you move toward pleasure and safety and away from distress and potential danger?

When your brain is flooded with dopamine, it's much harder for your PFC to kick in and do its logical thinking job. Research has shown that when dopamine levels are high, your ability to multitask and hold multiple competing ideas in mind is greatly reduced. So, in a dopamine-induced state, you'll be more likely to mistake a false alarm for a true dangerous situation and miss out on the opportunity to teach your brain how strong and competent you are. And as you now know, the more your brain thinks you're vulnerable, the more often and intensely it will sound the danger alarm in the future, and the more anxiety you'll continue to experience.

Unfortunately, this whole process also feeds negative beliefs about ourselves. You may start to think, *I must avoid discomfort because I can't handle it* (even though you really can) or *I'm weak* (even though you aren't), because your belief that you're unable to sit with those feelings has been strengthened over time. Your brain is mistaken and simply feeding off what it has learned from the many times you tried to avoid uncomfortable feelings.

The good news is that your emotional brain is not the only show in town. Your PFC is also responsible for directing which behaviors and situations you choose to face or avoid. You can train and strengthen your PFC so it can serve as a resiliency coach that guides you through uncomfortable and distressing situations.

The brain rewiring exercises in this chapter will help your PFC more effectively guide you through challenging moments. Continued practice in working your "resiliency muscles" will allow your PFC to more rapidly access and broadcast the message "Yes, this situation you're facing is hard and uncomfortable, but you can handle it. You got this, even if your emotional brain is telling you otherwise!"

We Are Not All Born Equally Resilient

Why is it that some people seem to move through challenging situations with ease while others seem to fall apart when confronted by similar difficulties? The answer is genetics, past experiences, and beliefs about ourselves and certain situations.

Let's first focus on what you come into the world with: genes. Research on the way babies react to the world around them tells us that we are all born with varying levels of resiliency. Some babies will barely make a peep when they are hungry or tired, while others wail in agony at the slightest discomfort. Studies assessing how these more sensitive babies handle distress show changes in their heart rate, fearful or painful emotional expressions, and lots of trying to move away. Highly sensitive children often feel more easily over-whelmed in situations that are complex, unfamiliar, or have too much going on.

Environment Interacting with Biology

As you can see, from early on your genetic makeup influences how you react to discomfort or novelty. As you have grown and interacted with people and your environment, your experiences have continued to shape your resiliency abilities. If you grew up in an environment where you were gently pushed and were encouraged to work your way through age-appropriate challenges, you may have already been doing the hard work of teaching your brain it can handle being uncomfortable. In contrast, if you grew up in an environment where you were either frequently "rescued" from situations that your brain considered too difficult, or one where you were pushed too aggressively to "get over it" without your discomfort being acknowledged, you may have had fewer environmental opportunities to rewire your brain to become resilient.

No matter what your starting point, now is as good a time as any to begin to teach your brain just how hearty and competent it is. The first step in rewiring your brain to become resilient is to remind it and yourself of how much discomfort you already move through on a daily basis. It's common to put emotional pain on a pedestal, as something that must be avoided at all costs. But in reality, emotional pain is no different than physical pain. It serves its function by sending a signal that something noteworthy occurred, and you should proceed with caution. From this viewpoint, let's consider how much discomfort you've been able to handle throughout the course of your life and what this tells you about your ability to manage life's less-than-ideal moments.

Exercise #13: You Can Handle Discomfort

Useful for: Rewiring a brain that doesn't like feeling uncomfortable and is scared of emotional discomfort.

Time needed: Just a few moments of reflection

Go somewhere quiet where you can really focus on this rewiring. Think of all the uncomfortable feelings you experience on a frequent basis. In the last month, recall if you've had any of these feelings:

- Feeling hot

- Feeling cold

- Paper cut

- Headache or migraine

- Stubbed toe

- Bumped head

- Cold or flu

- Broken or sprained bone

- Food poisoning

- Getting a shot

- Dental work

- Discomfort during or after a hard workout

☞ *Were you strong enough to tolerate the discomfort of these feelings and move forward in your life?*

Next time you stub your toe or have any other form of physical discomfort, scan your body and really hone in on what it feels like to be having these difficult feelings. And the next time you're feeling emotional pain, do the same. How are they different? How are they the same? Journal your main takeaways.

How Is This Exercise Rewiring Your Brain?

When you learn to recognize and identify emotional pain as just another category of discomfort you frequently experience and effectively manage on a daily basis, you're rewiring your brain to realize how resilient it already is.

This exercise will teach your brain that it need not put emotional discomfort on a pedestal and treat it as too powerful to be challenged. You're rewiring your brain to see emotional discomfort as just another form of incoming data that can teach you something and help you move forward more effectively.

WHEN EMOTIONAL PAIN BECOMES LONG-TERM SUFFERING

Emotional pain transforms into long-term suffering when you turn away and try to avoid that which is inevitable and already unfolding. Similar to running as fast as you can in an attempt to outrun your own brain, with each step you take, there you still are. And as you're trying to outrun your emotional pain, your amygdala will be right there with you, attempting to do its job of sending you what your brain has determined to be an important message. And as you try to hide from this pain-based message, your brain sends a louder and more intense signal to make sure you receive it.

Imagine your good friend was about to take a sip of a delicious-looking drink and you knew it was laced with poison. How desperately would you try to communicate to them that they needed to immediately put the drink down? And imagine that as you were attempting to let them know they were in danger, they started running away from you and covering their ears and refusing to acknowledge your attempts at warning them. Wouldn't you speak louder and more urgently so your friend hears your message?

When you try to avoid or outrun your emotional pain, your brain will keep upping the signal in order to assist you with survival. Unfortunately, this creates a vicious cycle:

Emotional pain → Avoidance → More emotional pain → More avoidance = Increased long-term suffering

CATASTROPHIC BELIEFS ABOUT EMOTIONAL DISTRESS

As we've talked about, it's common to feel more equipped to handle physical than emotional discomfort. The teens we work with will often review all the uncomfortable physical conditions they'd rather have to endure if it would mean no longer having to deal with anxiety. In a recent session one teen said, "If only I could be struggling with a broken leg or even a faulty heart instead of this awful anxiety. Anything would be better than feeling this terrible."

If you fear and avoid emotional discomfort much more than physical discomfort, it's likely you hold catastrophic beliefs about the experience of emotional pain.

These common catastrophic beliefs are *all* inaccurate:

- Beliefs about how emotional distress will impact functioning

  I'll lose it (or lose control).

  I won't be able to function or cope if I allow myself to feel the pain.

- Beliefs about how bad the emotional discomfort will be

  I'm not going to survive this.

  This is (or will be) awful.

- Beliefs about your ability to handle emotional distress

  I can't handle it.

  The pain is unbearable.

- Beliefs about the permanence of emotional pain

  I'll never feel better.

  This is my new normal.

- Beliefs regarding external judgments of emotional pain

  Others will judge me as weak for feeling so bad.

  I can't be around people when I am feeling this bad.

The challenge with holding these beliefs is that they enhance the amygdala's fear response to any situation that may bring on uncomfortable emotions. When your PFC sends these catastrophic messages to your amygdala, it reacts fearfully, assuming you must be in danger; otherwise why would you be internally screaming something along the lines of "This is awful! I can't deal!"? And as you know, when your amygdala determines you're in danger, it initiates the fight-flight-freeze response, which is super helpful when running from a wild animal but unhelpful and utterly uncomfortable when dealing with missing your bus or misplacing your favorite shirt.

🔖 or 💻
Exercise #14: Challenge Your Catastrophic Beliefs About Emotional Discomfort

Useful for: Rewiring a brain that frequently makes extreme and anxiety-provoking predictions about how hard an upcoming challenge will be.

Time needed: Throughout the day

Now that you're more aware of the catastrophic beliefs fueling your fear of emotional distress, it's time to start offering yourself a more realistic assessment of the challenges you are facing. By providing yourself with a more realistic prediction of what you must manage, and your ability to do so, you'll rewire your brain to revise the messaging your PFC is sending to your amygdala from "I can't handle this" to "This is hard, but I'll get through it." With this more balanced assessment, your amygdala will decrease the fight-flight-freeze response it's emitting, and you'll feel less anxious.

For the next day, notice the thoughts your brain offers up when facing a challenging moment. To keep a record of your brain's top picks throughout the day, download the worksheet at http://www.newharbinger.com/43768, or write them down in your journal.

First, describe the distressing situation. Observe and then write down all the catastrophic thoughts that surface. Next, rate your overall distress level on a scale from 1 to 10.

For each thought you wrote down, try offering up a more realistic prediction: a balanced, fact-based interpretation of the distressing situation and your ability to manage it. Rate your overall distress level again.

👉 *How did you feel when you accepted as truth all the catastrophic thoughts your PFC offered you when you faced distressing situations throughout the day?*

☞ *How did you feel after you offered yourself a more balanced, realistic assessment of the distressing situations you were experiencing?*

☞ *Did your amygdala calm down once your PFC began to offer less "gloom-and-doom" predictions of your ability to survive the challenges before you?*

How Is This Exercise Rewiring Your Brain?

This exercise helps you practice activating logical and more realistic thoughts about uncomfortable or new situations, and not dwell on the negatives. When your amygdala gets the new, more realistic message, you can react in a way that is based less on fear and more on what's actually going on. Once your PFC reframes the situation with its logic, your amygdala also gets the message that it can handle the uncomfortable (but not red-alert) situation—you're rewiring your brain to more easily activate your PFC to think up more realistic predictions of a situation that might initially sound off the alarm in your amygdala. With these realistic predictions, you're better equipped to calm down your amygdala's fear alarm and proceed with tackling the situation ahead of you.

SEEK OUT THE DISCOMFORT

To strengthen your resilience, it's important to practice this skill not just when a difficult moment naturally arises but also to look for extra practice opportunities. Yes, you read that correctly. We are in fact encouraging you to make your life slightly more difficult. By doing this work, you'll further rewire your brain to build up immunity to discomfort. Intentionally exposing yourself to frustration is like being vaccinated. When you get a vaccine, you're exposing your body to a small dose of a virus or bacteria. After the vaccination, your body will use all its natural germ-fighting tools to get over the infection. Once your body learns to fight off this infection, your immune system remembers what it learned about how to protect you against that disease in the future. Similarly, by providing your brain with bite-size *resiliency challenges*, it will quickly learn and remember that it can handle life's harder moments.

Exercise #15: Train Your Brain to Become More Resilient

Useful for: Rewiring a brain that instantly protests at anything difficult or unpleasant.

Time needed: Fifteen minutes for Parts A and B. Part C will be repeated daily for ten days.

Part A: In your journal, jot down different aspects of life that make you frustrated or annoyed; for example, *being late, embarrassing myself, getting stains on my favorite clothing, having to listen to my mom's awful music in the car*, and so on. Try to think of at least ten.

Part B: For each item, try to come up with an exercise that will bring on a moderate level of distress—around a 5 on a scale of 1 to 10—and predict your distress. These examples can help you with this part of the exercise:

- Being late—Arriving at soccer practice five minutes late (predicted distress: 6)

- Embarrassing myself—Making myself trip when I go into a store where I'm not likely to see anyone I know (predicted distress: 4)

- Getting stains on my favorite clothing—Putting a tiny dot of ink on one of my favorite T-shirts (predicted distress: 6)

- Having to listen to my mom's awful music in the car—Forcing myself to listen for five minutes, instead of immediately putting in earbuds (predicted distress: 5)

Part C: For the next ten days, your job is to do one challenge a day for a total of ten. Use your journal to jot down your thoughts, feeling, and reactions. As you do each challenge, note your actual distress level, and compare it to your predicted distress level. Overall, was it higher or lower? Did you notice any patterns? Were some challenges easier than you predicted and others more difficult?

How Is This Exercise Rewiring Your Brain?

This exercise activates your PFC and amygdala to strengthen the resilience network of your brain. When you actively seek out discomfort, your brain will learn that emotional distress is not "the enemy." There's no threat to survival here—you're still safe! Through these repeated experiences of willingly feeling uncomfortable, your brain learns to break the cycle of reacting to potential emotional distress by sounding the fear alarm, which only brings on more of that emotional distress you were trying to avoid in the first place. By doing this exercise, you're rewiring your brain to not react so intensely, but instead to learn that it can handle uncomfortable feelings and difficult situations.

☞ *On a scale from 1 to 10, rate how motivated you are to continue working on rewiring your brain to be resilient and effective at moving past and through difficult situations.*

KEY TAKEAWAYS

In this chapter, you learned that people are not born equally resilient, but that you can always rewire your brain to better handle life's difficult moments (no matter what your starting point is). By doing this work, you're training your brain to understand how strong and competent you truly are. Your brain has been able to grasp this important lesson not by lecturing it about how strong and good it is, but instead by having it experience this truth by taking on small doses of uncomfortable feelings and challenging situations—and surviving them!

You now have the tools and training to effectively and efficiently move through and past life's challenging moments. You now understand how emotional suffering is increased by fighting against the built-in pain that is inevitably part of the human experience, and how you can reduce your emotional suffering by opening up and accepting discomfort rather than fighting it.

CHAPTER 6

Rewire Your Brain to Shift Perspectives

The fourth-period bell rang and everyone flooded into the hallway, making their way toward lockers, friends, and fifth-period classes. Michael got a rush of energy as he exchanged grins with several friends, and even caught his crush's eye. He noticed that one of his buddies wasn't making eye contact as they passed, but didn't think much of it, assuming his friend was just distracted by an upcoming test.

Lisa, meanwhile, felt a wave of hostility as she walked down that same hall. She saw frowning faces and judgment, and she swore she heard some girls whispering her name as she passed. As her crush approached, he stared at his phone screen. Lisa's stomach sank with rejection, and she completely missed when he looked up a moment later and waved. She tried to make conversation with a friend outside her next class, but the friend didn't smile and barely responded. Lisa's stomach tied into knots as she worried about why her friend was mad at her.

What's happening here? Is it that Michael is just more popular, and Lisa doesn't have as many friends? Nope. The difference is that

Michael generally has what we call a *positive bias*, meaning his brain tends to notice positive information over negative, and he doesn't interpret neutral information as negative. He immediately noticed smiling faces and didn't take it personally when one friend seemed distant. By contrast, Lisa has a more *negative bias*. Influenced by her anxious mood, she noticed all the potentially negative things around her and missed the positive ones. Unlike Michael, Lisa takes ambiguous events very personally and negatively; for example, assuming her friend was angry when she didn't smile. In fact, her friend was feeling stressed about her own home life, as her dad had been drinking more and more lately. It had nothing to do with Lisa, but Lisa didn't know that, and assumed the worst. Her anxiety only got worse from there.

NEGATIVE BIASES AND THE BRAIN

Did you know that we are actually evolutionarily hardwired to jump to the negative and miss the positive? Think about our caveman ancestors—their lives depended on their ability to scope out the negative (potentially life-ending!) things around them. Their survival rates increased when they paid attention to the saber-toothed tiger instead of the bush of juicy berries the tiger was hiding behind. And even after years and years of our brains evolving, we still have that old bias: we tend to pay more attention to potential threats. Of course, some of us, like Lisa, have more of a bias toward threats than others do, like Michael.

Today, we generally don't need to be as alert for immediate, life-ending threats. Because our modern brains are more sophisticated, our higher-order cognitive processes (in particular the PFC) take the negative information and try to make sense of it, rather than immediately reacting. The downside is that for some of us, our brains seem to run off with stories of what the negatives mean about us and the world around us in a way that's not helpful, given that there's no serious threat to our safety.

The good news is that there is another way. You can rewire your brain to pay less attention to false alarms and more attention to positive information by engaging in exercises that shift your focus from the bad to the good. In turn, you'll feel less anxious. In fact, research on this sort of rewiring exercise has shown that the left side of your PFC is more activated after you practice shifting your attention to positives in a way that is conscious and frequent. So, with practice, you can start to change your mental habits! With more attention to the positives, you get to take in meaningful interactions with friends, family, pets, and yourself without getting caught up in fear and self-doubt. You can focus on what's going well and feel more confident.

Before we jump into the exercises that will help you focus more on the positive and lower your anxiety, it's helpful to review some more of the science from this area.

Research has shown again and again that when people are anxious, they're more likely to fixate on negative information, ignore positive information, and even interpret neutral information as negative (thanks a lot, caveman ancestors!). A classic example comes from studies in which research participants were presented with pictures of different faces. Anxious people were more likely to focus on the single negative facial expression among many positive ones. The really interesting data comes from the neutral facial expressions, though. Anxious people were more likely to interpret neutral faces as upset or threatening, and nonanxious people were more likely to say the faces were neutral or even positive—for instance, saying the person looked calm. You can imagine the effects these biases have on daily life, as you move through the halls, talk with people on the bus, give a speech in a class, or get feedback from a teacher.

You might be thinking, *Isn't it kind of delusional to ignore the negative and just focus on the positive? Negative information is important and real. I don't want to be some shallow person who just thinks everything is happy and doesn't see what's really going on.*

To this we say, good call! We're right there with you. Negative information *can* be very important and real. If a bear is about to jump out of the woods and attack you, you wouldn't want to convince yourself the rustling in the bushes is definitely, without any doubt, coming from a squirrel. And if your friends are truly upset at you, you wouldn't want to walk around giving high fives and assuming nothing is wrong. As therapists, we feel we have an ethical duty to be honest with our clients, and we never want to deceive anyone.

The key point to keep in mind here is that if you're anxious, the odds are very high that you tend to be *too* negative in terms of how you process information. You're probably more like Lisa than Michael, missing out on the positive information even when it's really there, such as when Lisa didn't notice her crush wave, and misreading an ambiguous situation, like a friend who seems upset, as something negative and personal to you.

Is it possible to ensure that you process all information exactly accurately, never interpreting something as too negative or too positive? Of course not. Your anxiety would love it if you could be that certain, but life just doesn't work that way.

Instead, you have to consider how your life has been going for you so far. Are you more anxious than you'd like to be? Do you think you tend to fixate on negative information? If so, the odds are much higher that you're missing positive information than ignoring negative information. You're always the one in control, but we bet that by challenging your own negative biases, you'll find that you feel less anxious and more grounded, and even like you're able to *more* accurately assess the world around you than you were before.

Common Negative Biases

There are many other negative biases that anxious people tend to struggle with, often without realizing it. This list includes some of the common ones, taken from teens we've helped overcome anxiety:

- Obsessing over something negative a friend said

- Beating yourself up for missing a question on a test

- Focusing on a time you missed a shot/goal/pass or lost a game

- Taking a friend's silence personally and assuming the friend is mad at you

- Fixating on a time your parents fought with each other, worrying it means they will get divorced

- Feeling rejected when your crush doesn't seem interested in you

- Suspecting that people are gossiping and saying negative things about you

The next three exercises all involve your negative biases. To complete them, you can use your journal or download the worksheets provided at http://www.newharbinger.com/43768, where you'll also find completed samples.

📕 or 💻
Exercise #16a: Identify Your Negative Biases

Useful for: Rewiring a brain that needs some extra help noticing when it focuses on the negatives and skips the positives.

Time needed: About ten minutes

Draw three lines down a page, dividing it into four even columns. In the first column, make a list of your negative biases: the ways you tend to focus on the negative in your own life. Include any of the common ones you just read, and add others that are accurate for you. Try to list as many as you can think of. Leave the other three columns blank for now.

How Is This Exercise Rewiring Your Brain?

When you can better see what your negative biases are, you're increasing your awareness of the way your brain interprets situations in which you feel anxiety. The wiring of your PFC is strengthened when you put into place your more advanced thinking skills as you work to also identify missing positive information. By doing this exercise, you're rewiring your brain to better catch on to when your negativity bias is taking charge.

☞ *On a scale of 1 to 10, rate how much it's a priority for you to continue to work on calling out your negativity bias.*

📖 or 💻
Exercise #16b: Challenge Your Negative Biases

Useful for: Rewiring a brain that often interprets situations and events as negative.

Time needed: Ten to fifteen minutes

For this exercise, continue with the worksheet you created in your journal or downloaded for exercise #16a. In the first column, you should have already listed some of the negative biases from your life. In the second column, list at least one effect each negative bias has on your life.

For example, for the negative bias "Obsessing over something negative a friend said," you might come up with some of the following effects:

- Feel anxious

- Spend time reviewing past conversations with that friend in my head

- Get so distracted it's harder to focus on my schoolwork, and sometimes get worse grades

- Have a hard time falling asleep because I'm anxious about what my friend said

- Have less fun when I'm around my friends, because I'm feeling worried and don't want to make things worse

- Snap at my parents, because I'm feeling stressed about my friend

If you can come up with more (and we bet you can!), that's even better. Now, in the third column, list at least one way in which your life would be different if you challenged each cognitive bias. As a hint, you might look at the previous column, and consider how those things could be flipped. For instance, you might come up with:

- Feel less anxious

- Spend less time reviewing past conversations with my friend in my head, and more time doing things I enjoy

- Be able to focus better on my schoolwork, and get better grades

- Fall asleep more easily

- Have more fun around my friends

- Argue less with my parents, because I'm less on edge

If you get stuck at any point, you might pause to ask yourself, *What would I tell a friend if she were in this situation?* For example, if you knew that your friend obsessed so much over negative comments by another friend that she lost sleep and had less fun hanging out with everyone, you could tell her that if she could challenge this negative bias she might sleep better and enjoy being around her friend group more. We're often better at giving advice to others than to ourselves, so this can be a good coping skill when you're feeling stuck.

Of course, if you get stuck, you could also always go and *actually ask a friend* what they think! Show them the exercise, and have them weigh in on the parts you're having a hard time with. You might see if they want to do the exercise for their own life, too, and return the favor by helping them. Everyone experiences *some* negative biases. Doing this exercise with a friend can help you not only understand yours more clearly but also help you feel less alone.

How Is This Exercise Rewiring Your Brain?

You are using the logical part of your brain to identify how your life would be different if you challenged your biases, setting yourself up for less emotional reactivity. Bringing your attention to negative biases demands use of your PFC and signals to your amygdala that it needs to slow down. Here, you can start to retrain your brain to strengthen the pathways that strike a better balance between logic and emotion in these mind messages.

Your PFC is also home to super helpful skills, like planning, organization, memory, attention, and self-regulation, which are part of a skill set known as executive function skills. When you pause to not only think about challenging biases but also how life could be different, you're putting these skills to use. By doing this exercise, you're rewiring your brain to incorporate the use of logic and reasoning to think long term, and not let in-the-moment emotion tell you how to live your life.

Think back to your emotional brain (amygdala) and your thinking brain (PFC). You've learned that sometimes your emotion overrides your logic, which makes it harder to enjoy and partake fully in your life. Remember, when you experience false alarms, your emotions override your rational thoughts, and your PFC can't quite put its logic to use. But the real goal here is to make both communicate with each other.

In a truly threatening situation, you still need your amygdala activated so you can feel fear *and* you need your PFC to help you think logically so you can get to safety. Your PFC and amygdala provide each other with helpful information, but the PFC's logical messages to the amygdala ("Your friend might not be smiling at you because she's stressed about something in her own life.") is not as quick as the amygdala's emotional message to the PFC ("Your friend is mad at you for something you did.").

We know this is especially true for teens. In a study where teens and adults had to identify emotions of faces, brain scans showed that teens were more likely to rely on their amygdalae to process their perception of emotion, while adults used their PFCs. Interestingly, the teens mostly answered incorrectly! They misperceived the emotion on the face as shocked or angry, rather than the correct answer, fear (and we hate to say it, but the adults mostly got it right!). But as the teens grew older, researchers found that they began to shift away from instinctive amygdala activation and toward reasoning in the PFC.

☞ *On a scale of 1 to 10, rate how much it's a priority for you to continue to work on rewiring your brain to see the whole picture.*

📖 or 💻
Exercise #16c: Identify Your Negativity Hot Spots

Useful for: Rewiring a brain that automatically sends negative thoughts in certain situations.

Time needed: About ten minutes

The next step to challenging negative biases is to recognize where they're most likely to happen, so that you can go into these hot spots armed with a plan. In the last column of your journal or the worksheet you downloaded, write down the hot spots where the bias most often pops up. In this case, a "spot" can be a person, place, or anything else that frequently triggers the negative bias.

For example, you might notice that you sometimes obsess over negative comments made by other people, but this actually only happens with a particular friend or a certain teacher. In that case, having a conversation with that friend or teacher would be the hot spot where you'd want to be on the lookout for negative biases. You might notice that whenever you walk past a certain group of girls in the hallway, it's a hot spot where you become worried they're talking about you. Or you might even recognize your negative biases tend to get really bad when you haven't slept well in a while. Waking up tired would be your sign that you're in a hot spot.

How Is This Exercise Rewiring Your Brain?

Your brain stores past experiences in your long-term memory so that next time you encounter a similar experience, you're prepped with the important information in the quickest way possible. As a result, your PFC is wired for you to be primed, or in automatic mode, for feeling a certain way or doing a certain thing based on that information about specific situations.

And before you know it, you might be in one of your hot spots. Knowing your hot spots helps rewire your brain to slow down this automatic process of jumping to the negative. You separate your actual, present-moment experience from what your past experiences and negativity bias are warning you. That way, you can beat your negativity bias before it hijacks your experience. By doing this exercise, you're rewiring your brain to better call out your negativity bias in the places it likes to hang out most.

☞ *On a scale of 1 to 10, rate how much it's a priority for you to continue to work on calling out your negativity bias.*

Now that you know some of your personal negative biases, how they impact your life, and where they're most likely to occur, what should you do to challenge them? The key step—and this tiny trick can go a long way toward reducing your anxiety—is to pause and identify a single piece of positive information you might have missed.

The goal here is not to sugarcoat the situation, convincing yourself that something is more positive than it really is, but rather to recognize that as someone with anxiety, you're prone to fixate on the negative to a disproportionate extent. You want to challenge this tendency.

The amazing part, as we'll explain, is that you don't even have to *believe* the positive information for it to help. The simple act of challenging the negative automatic process will help transform your neural circuitry and allow you to view things in a more balanced, realistic light.

Exercise #17: Challenge Your Negative Biases

Useful for: Rewiring a brain that has trouble talking back to its negative thoughts.

Time needed: Twenty minutes

Turn to the list of common negative biases earlier in this chapter. For each one, come up with something positive our clients might have missed when they focused on the negative. For example, for "Obsessing over something negative a friend said," you could say that the friend likely also said at least some positive things during the conversation. Or maybe the friend *was* trying to say something mean, but it was because she was just jealous. Now that you see how this works, try applying this process to each of the remaining examples on the list.

Note: *You don't need to write down your answers unless it's helpful. We've listed some possible answers following this exercise, but there is no right answer. The important thing is for you to warm up your brain on your own before checking our answers.*

Once you're done warming up, go back to the worksheet you completed in exercises 16a–c, and think of positives you might have missed. Going forward, each time one of the negative thoughts pops into your head, challenge yourself to remember the positive information you came up with. And each time that you go into a hot spot where you're likely to experience negative biases in the future, prepare yourself to be (1) looking out for the biases, and then (2) stopping to identify some positive information that you missed.

Once you learn this exercise, we encourage you to use it on an ongoing basis.

How Is This Exercise Rewiring Your Brain?

The best way to overcome your tendency toward negative biases is to challenge them, even briefly. When you do this, your amygdala quiets down and your PFC springs into action, offering your brain some perspective. Even if that perspective doesn't seem like a reasonable explanation, it decreases the emotional intensity and panic you might feel from your negative perspective. Having multiple ideas (even for a brief moment!) rewires your brain to activate your PFC and strengthen more neural pathways that can rewire you to see things differently next time.

☞ *On a scale of 1 to 10, rate how much it's a priority for you to continue to work on talking back to negative thoughts.*

Possible positive answers:

- **Beating yourself up for missing a question on a test**
  The teen might have gotten a high score despite having missed one question, or might have passed many other tests.

Talking with the teacher about the missed problem could actually strengthen their relationship and help the teen get a better overall grade in the class.

- **Focusing on a time you missed a shot/goal/pass or lost a game**

  The teen could think about all the shots/goals/passes she made, or about all the games her team won. Even if she hasn't been making shots/goals/passes, she might focus on other aspects of her physical performance that have improved, such as her ability to run faster.

- **Taking a friend's silence personally and assuming the friend is mad at you**

  It could be that the friend is distracted by something going on in their own life, and is in no way mad at the teen we worked with. It's possible that the friend is giving the "silent treatment" because she is feeling jealous. It's possible the friend doesn't even realize she's acting "weird."

- **Fixating on a time your parents fought with each other, worrying it means they will get divorced**

  The parents are still married. They were recently hugging and chose to do an activity together. Healthy fighting is an important part of communication in relationships and can actually be a sign that people trust each other enough to express their true opinions. Even if they did divorce, there are lots of happy, healthy divorced families.

- **Feeling rejected when your crush doesn't seem interested in you**

  The teen we worked with may have missed all the positive signs his crush sent, like smiling or trying to strike up conversation. It's possible that the crush is interested, and because of that feels especially shy around the teen. Maybe the crush really isn't interested in this teen, but this will ultimately be a good thing, because it will free him up to begin dating someone who is a much better fit.

- **Suspecting that people are gossiping and saying negative things about you**

  It's possible the people were talking about the teen we worked with, but actually said something positive. More likely, they weren't talking about the teen at all. It's hard to "disprove" something that happened in the past, but in the future, the teen we worked with found it helpful to notice positive things during conversations with people she worried would gossip—like when they smiled, or laughed at a joke she made, or made good eye contact. All this positive information made our client feel less "paranoid" about being gossiped about later on.

KEY TAKEAWAYS

If you're anxious, you probably have some biases that cause you to fixate on negative events, ignore positive ones, and even interpret neutral events as negative. In order to rewire your brain to be less anxious, taking in a more balanced view of the world, practice getting to know your biases and your hot spots, and then notice at least some of the positive information you've been ignoring.

CHAPTER 7

Rewire Your Brain to Dial Down Intense Emotions

Alexandra's parents asked her to drive her younger brother Bo to school for a few days while they were away on vacation. Alexandra had been dreading this task for weeks. Although they went to the same school, she had to be there by a quarter to eight, and Bo didn't have to arrive until eight. Also, she believed Bo might be the slowest human being on the planet. He walked at a snail's pace, tied his shoes like a toddler, and was perpetually disorganized. Getting out the door with him felt like walking through a tornado, with papers and objects flying around.

On the first morning of her parents' vacation, Alexandra tried to wake Bo up early to give him extra time for his chaos. If it was at all possible, he seemed to be moving at an even slower pace than normal. Alexandra felt like he was intentionally trying to drive her crazy. She followed him around the house yelling for him to move faster. The louder she yelled, the slower he moved. By seven thirty, she was full-on screaming at him. How could her parents have left her with this impossible task? Her blood felt like it was boiling, and all she could think about was how much she despised Bo and her selfish parents, who cared only about themselves. She felt as though she were trapped in a black hole of misery. In that moment, everything felt utterly wrong. She was overwhelmed by her emotions of anger, anxiety, and despair. She didn't know how to move forward and fix the current situation, or the day, and basically what felt like her entire life. She had tried so hard to get everything right and yet, as usual, everything felt wrong. On some level, she knew she was overreacting and that even if she was a few minutes late to school, it wouldn't be the end of the world, but she couldn't shake that feeling of rage. Alexandra wished she could go back to bed and just wake up as a new person who either didn't have the slowest brother in the world or was actually equipped to handle life's frustrating moments.

Olivia, too, had been assigned the same dreaded task of driving her sister Allie to school while her parents were out of town. Olivia also planned how to get Allie out the door as efficiently as possible. When Olivia tried to wake Allie, her sister pulled her blanket over her head and screamed that she had time to sleep for five more minutes. Though extremely frustrated, Olivia took a moment to take a deep breath and review her options. She could (1) yell at Allie to wake up, (2) call their mom and dad, or (3) keep getting herself ready for the next five minutes until Allie woke up. She also thought about the consequences for each. Yelling would lead to Allie purposely staying in bed longer, which would make them even more late. Calling their mom and dad would disrupt them on their vacation, bother Allie, and take up even more time—which would also make them late. Getting herself ready until Allie woke up seemed like the best way to get them out of the house on time, so she decided to go with plan 3.

Do you relate more to how Alexandra or Olivia handled the frustrating task of needing to drive their siblings to school? One way to think through this question is to review a difficult moment you've experienced in the past few weeks. Assess how much distress and discomfort it caused you. Next, think of a friend or family member you consider a pretty balanced, reasonable person. How do you imagine they would handle the same situation?

YOUR TRIGGER-HAPPY AMYGDALA

Why do some people seem to move through challenging situations with ease and grace while others lose their cool so rapidly? As discussed, people who experience higher levels of anxiety tend to have trigger-happy amygdalae. They are quicker to startle and react more intensely to potential threats. Struggling with out-of-control anxiety is a sign your amygdala is overwhelming your PFC. So much information floods your brain all at once about any and all potential threats that your whole brain feels jammed up. It's like having too many windows open on your computer or too many apps running at the same time on your phone. Trying to manage processing all that information at once tends to be inefficient and ineffective.

So the first step in being better able to navigate an emotionally charged situation is to learn how to calm down your amygdala. Once your amygdala takes it down a notch, your PFC can take over and apply effective problem-solving skills. The billion dollar question is, how can you calm down your amygdala?

Pop quiz: My life experience has taught me that an effective way to calm down my amygdala is to

A.   scream at myself to CALM DOWN!

B.   avoid the topic or situation that is bothering me.

C.   take a deep breath and then do a yoga pose.

D.   none of the above

If you answered D, congratulations! You're one step closer to being the proud owner of a calmer amygdala. For different reasons, none of the most frequently used strategies (options A, B, and C) are effective at reassuring your amygdala that you're safe and sound. This chapter is going to teach you how to hack into your nervous system to turn off the fight-flight-freeze response, and turn on the "rest-and-digest" response. By learning how to dial down your body's functioning, you'll have access to a remote for your brain and be able to turn down the volume and intensity of your anxiety and other uncomfortable emotions.

THE MIND-BODY CONNECTION

You can change the signal your body sends your amygdala by taking advantage of your mind-body connection. Your nervous system is a network of nerves and cells that rapidly exchanges information between parts of your body. Your brain and spinal cord are part of the central nervous system, while your peripheral nervous system consists of the nerves found throughout your body. Within the peripheral nervous system is the autonomic nervous system, which includes both the sympathetic and the parasympathetic systems. The autonomic system controls key bodily functions such as heart rate, digestion, and breathing. Some of these physiological responses are activated in opposite ways depending on the situation: the sympathetic nervous system activates your body for fight-flight-freeze mode, and the parasympathetic nervous system activates your body for rest-and-digest mode.

When your amygdala senses you're in danger, it activates your sympathetic nervous system and turns on all the bodily functions—such as increasing your oxygen intake and heart rate—that would help you flee a burning building, or any attempt to survive any other life-threatening situation. The job of your parasympathetic nervous system (a.k.a. your rest-and-digest system), is to conserve energy and manage your bodily functions when you're in nonthreatening situations. Together your sympathetic and parasympathetic nervous systems act like the accelerator and brakes on a car. Your sympathetic system is the accelerator that gets you fired up, and your parasympathetic system is the brake that slows you down.

At this point, we imagine you're more familiar with the power of your sympathetic (fight-flight-freeze) nervous system than with the calming abilities of your parasympathetic (rest-and-digest) nervous system. This chapter is going to provide you with tools and exercises to turn on your parasympathetic nervous system. By calming down your body, you'll send a signal to your amygdala that the coast is clear and you're not in danger. Once your amygdala chills out, your PFC will be able to run the show and initiate effective problem solving to guide you through challenging terrain.

CALM DOWN YOUR BODY TO CALM DOWN YOUR BRAIN

In the first few sessions of anxiety treatment, we always ask teens what strategies they've already tried to manage their symptoms. One of the most common responses we hear is "I tried relaxation exercises like yoga and meditation, but they didn't work." In fact, many teens tell us that trying to relax only made them feel more anxious. We call this phenomena "relaxation-induced anxiety." If an armed gunman were standing beside you, and he shouted that he'd shoot unless you calm down, how would you feel? How likely would it be that you'd be able to get your body to relax? When you feel desperate to relax or calm down, of course you only end up feeling more anxious. But, if you can adopt an open and flexible attitude and tell yourself, *I'd like to calm down, but I'm not in danger if I don't (or can't)*, you're one step closer to activating your parasympathetic nervous system and turning on the relaxation response.

Slow Breathing: The Volume Dial for Your Emotions

The most powerful and readily accessible tool you have to calm your mind and body is your breath. By slowing down your breath, you activate your parasympathetic (rest-and-digest) nervous system. All you need to do to move past anxiety's false alarm is to engage in five minutes of slow breathing, sending the signal to your brain: "We're not in danger so there's no reason to breathe so rapidly and fuel up with all this extra oxygen. There's no need to run and no one to fight, so less oxygen is required to manage this moment. Small, gentle breaths are all we need."

Some people find that their brains quickly wander to different topics, or that the very act of focusing on the breath makes them so hyperaware of this activity that their breathing becomes forced and tight. If you notice you're struggling with either of these problems, it may be helpful to use the sensations of your rising and falling breath as a sensory cue to keep you focused.

📱 or 💻
Exercise #18: Slow Breathe Past Anxious Moments

Useful for: Rewiring a brain that could use some help dialing down physical symptoms of anxiety.

Time needed: Five minutes twice a day for a week

Part A: Find a quiet place where you can focus your attention on your breath. For the next week, practice slow breathing twice a day, once in the morning and once in the evening, for five minutes, using a timer (your phone would work great!).

1. Slowly breathe in for three seconds, resting your hand gently on your stomach. As your hand rises, slowly count to 1 ... 2 ... 3 .... Picture the air rising through your body, from your belly upward toward your brain, filling your brain with a fresh dose of oxygen.

2. Gently hold your breath for three seconds, 1 ... 2 ... 3 ....

3. Slowly breathe out for three seconds, 1 ... 2 ... 3 .... Notice your hand on your stomach falling and your lips gently pursed as your mouth slowly releases air. Picture the oxygen moving

slowly from the top of your head, slowly through making its way down your body to the soles of your feet.

4.   Gently hold your breath for three seconds, 1 ... 2 ... 3 ....

5.   Repeat.

Using your journal or the worksheet you can download at http://www.newharbinger.com/43768, rate your anxiety on a scale from 1 to 10 before and after, and add any notes about your experience.

Part B: Now, it's time to take this slow breathing tool on the road. Use it whenever you notice your amygdala overreacting to a situation and determining you're in mortal danger when in reality you're simply facing a modern-life challenge. The next time you feel extreme emotions, practice five minutes of slow breathing. You'll find that your body and mind settle down after this time-out.

Again, download the worksheet at http://www.newharbinger.com/43768, or use your journal. For the next week, fill out the log every time you have an anxious or stressed moment and then engage in five minutes of slow breathing.

Releasing Tension from Your Nervous System

As you read earlier, when your amygdala senses you're in danger, it activates your sympathetic (fight-flight-freeze) nervous system, which makes your muscles naturally contract. Tight muscles serve to protect your vital organs, such as your heart, lungs, and kidneys, from external threats. The opposite is also true. When your amygdala determines that you're safe, it activates your parasympathetic (rest-and-digest) nervous system, so that your muscles are more relaxed (think: rag doll versus robot). Tensing your muscles requires a good deal of oxygen. For survival purposes, it's best not to waste precious energy tensing your muscles when there's no danger to run from or fight. When the coast is clear, it's more adaptive and efficient for your muscles to be relaxed.

These safety/danger signals travel both ways. Tense muscles send a signal to your amygdala that you're in danger. And relaxing your muscles signals your amygdala that you're safe and no external threats are present. This two-way information exchange offers you an opportunity to activate your parasympathetic nervous system on demand by learning how to relax your muscles.

Progressive Muscle Relaxation: The Pressure Valve for Your Nervous System

Progressive muscle relaxation (PMR) is another simple exercise you can use to calm down your nervous system. PMR entails tensing and relaxing all muscles in your body in an exaggerated way. If you have been experiencing anxiety for a while, chances are your body is very familiar with holding tension for extended periods of time but needs some training on how to shift gears and enter a state of physiological relaxation. By holding the tension in your body in an exaggerated fashion and then practicing releasing the tension, your brain will have an easier time noticing how different these two states feel. And from there your brain will be one step closer to being able to relax your muscles on demand, when you are most in need of tension relief.

Tense all the muscles in your body for fifteen seconds. Tense your fists. Tense your face. Tense your forehead, eyes, and mouth. Tense your shoulders and watch them rise. Tense your stomach.

Tense your thighs. Tense your calves. Tense your toes and notice them curl.

Now release all this tension. Imagine you're a rag doll or an overcooked piece of spaghetti. Imagine you're shaking off and releasing into the universe all the excess energy stored in your tense muscles. Perhaps roll your head around a bit or stretch your mouth or shake out your hands. Do whatever it takes for you to feel like you're switching from holding all your tension in your body to letting go of the tension and releasing it into the external world.

Repeat three times.

📖 or 💻
Exercise #19: Practice Progressive Muscle Relaxation

Useful for: Rewiring a brain that needs help dialing down physical tension in the body.

Time needed: Five minutes twice a day, once in the morning and once before bed, for a week

Just as critical as it is to practice PMR when you're feeling relatively calm, it's also important to practice applying PMR to high-stress situations when you could most benefit from this release of tension. At http://www.newharbinger.com/43768, you'll find a worksheet to fill out every time you have an anxious or stressed moment and then engage in PMR. Use a scale of 1 to 10 to rate your anxiety before and after.

You can also use your journal to keep track of how PMR affects your anxiety level.

How Are These Exercises Rewiring Your Brain?
By practicing slowing your breathing and relaxing your muscles, you're signaling to your amygdala that you're safe. This puts the

brakes on your amygdala's fight-flight-freeze response. Your heart rate decreases as it no longer needs to pump as fast to get blood to your muscles. When your brain realizes that you're choosing to forgo your armor of tense muscles, it figures out that there are no immediate threats that could harm you.

BODY AWARENESS TRAINING

Have you ever suddenly realized that you're sitting with your arms crossed tightly over your chest? Or that your jaw is clenched? People struggling with anxiety have a tendency to notice their bodies only when they're operating in full-stress mode. Learning how to observe and attend to your body before you melt down is critical.

Your body isn't simply a storage unit for anxious feelings. There's a lot more going on than just uncomfortable sensations. If you pay attention to it on a regular basis, it won't feel like it needs to scream and yell to get your attention.

Exercise #20: Attend to Your Nervous System Through a Body Scan

Useful for: Rewiring a brain that has the urge to quickly get rid of uncomfortable physical sensations.

Time needed: Five minutes

Take a moment to scan your body for all attention-grabbing sensations. Start with the top of your head. Notice any tension or tingling or heaviness in your scalp and forehead. Next, move down to your face, your mouth, your nose, your forehead, and your ears. Notice your shoulders. Are they raised and tight, loose, or somewhere in between? Next, notice your chest and any heaviness or tightness that may be present. Continue moving down to your stomach, your arms, your hands, the feeling of your legs making contact with the seat or floor, and, finally, your feet. Now, notice any urges that may be showing up to change or rid yourself of the sensations you're having. You may be experiencing the desire to feel more relaxed or less tense. You don't need to change anything. Your only job right now is to make room for whatever you're currently feeling.

For the next week, when you're in an enjoyable or neutral situation and feeling relatively calm, take a moment to pay attention to your body and do this scan. If you notice any excess tension, spend a minute doing progressive muscle relaxation or slow breathing.

CHANGE YOUR MIND'S CHANNEL

When things feel too hard, it's never a good time to sit around thinking. Thoughts that bubble up in these "hot" moments will be extreme and inaccurate representations of your actual situation. These are certainly *not* moments to make any big decisions or take any life-altering actions. The trick is to learn how to place your attention on the outside world. You can focus on the sky, on a chair, on your dog, or even on a speck of lint. It doesn't matter what you focus on as long as you are guiding your attention away from your extreme thoughts and feelings.

Getting your brain engaged in the current moment as quickly as possible allows it to take a break from tending to an extreme emotional reaction. Here are the top strategies the teens we work with use to change their channels from a nonstop "Gloom and Doom" marathon to the "Be Here Now" channel.

- **Engage your five senses.**

  Looking around you, describe at least one thing you notice with each of your five senses. For example, I *see* a big beautiful tree out the window; I *hear* buzzing, possibly from my air conditioner; I *taste* the sweetness of a ripe banana; I *smell* the laundry detergent from my T-shirt; I *feel* the soft texture of the couch as my arms touch it.

- **Change your temperature.**

  To change your temperature, you can hold an ice cube or take a hot or cold shower. You can go outside and feel a cold breeze or the warm air on your skin or the rain falling on your face. You can drink a cold drink or a hot drink.

- **Change your body positioning.**

  It's always helpful to change the position your body was in when your overwhelming feelings of anxiety first set in. For example, if you're sitting hunched over when you notice how stressed you're feeling, stand and stretch by extending your arms as far as they can go. If you're pacing around like your pants are on fire, sit down. If you're hiding in bed under the covers, stand up and do ten jumping jacks.

- **Change what you feel.**

  Instead of what you're touching, pet your dog or cat, or put on lotion and notice how your skin changes from feeling dry to feeling nourished, or play with Silly Putty or slime or some other fidget toy.

- **Change what you smell, taste, or hear.**

  To wake up your sense of smell, you could carry lavender oil or a favorite scent, or a lip balm or lotion with an appealing smell. Offer yourself a pleasant taste, like a mint, gum, or a small candy. To change the sound you're attending to, create a "Change My Mind's Channel" playlist.

We recommend using one or a combination of these strategies until you feel less consumed by a "hot" thought or feeling. The possibilities are endless, and you're welcome to add your own ideas.

Some of the teens we work with find it helpful to create notes in their phones listing their top three emotional regulation strategies— like speed bumps to help them slow down. It doesn't matter what form you choose when placing these emotional speed bumps throughout your life. What does matter is having external reminders to slow you down when your PFC is offline and your amygdala is running the show.

How Are These Exercises Rewiring Your Brain?

By shifting your attention to the present moment, your brain becomes less preoccupied with intense emotions. Your PFC sends the message to your brain that you don't have to get caught up in unhelpful thoughts or uncomfortable physical sensations. When you just notice your distress but don't do anything to lessen it, your amygdala learns that the intense emotion is just uncomfortable, but not dangerous. Focusing your efforts on more soothing sensations allows your brain to take some space from your amygdala's alarm signals and from unhelpful thoughts that keep you stuck in your intense and uncomfortable emotions.

KEY TAKEAWAYS

You now know how to use tools to help you turn down the volume of your extreme emotions. When every cell in your body is revved up and ready to fight, flee, or freeze, switching gears and activating your parasympathetic (rest-and-digest) nervous system can feel nearly impossible. But remember, just because it feels nearly impossible doesn't mean it is. The main challenge with using the emotional regulation tools you've learned is that moments of high emotion unfold very quickly. When your amygdala is running the show, it may not feel like you have the time or clarity to access your emotional brakes. Regular practice with these exercises can help you do just that and better dial down intense emotions and uncomfortable physical sensations.

CHAPTER 8

Rewire Your Brain to "Just Do It"

Sam and Noah were both taking an AP psychology class. On the first day, the professor reviewed the syllabus and told the class that there would be only a few weekly assignments; their grades for the course would be based mostly on their final projects.

Upon hearing the coursework requirements and their due dates, Sam breathed a sigh of relief. He knew it was going to be a busy semester given the other difficult classes he was taking and the part-time job he had recently started. He was glad that he'd be able to pace himself for this one class and that there wouldn't be a ton of work at the start. Sam put the final project out of his mind for the first two months of the semester until the professor asked the students to each give a brief update on their progress. When it was Sam's turn, he was able to stammer his way through a few sentences. After that, fear set in and he told himself it was time to get to work. He thought about how he could complete the project in time. He planned to dedicate a few hours a week for the next six weeks to stay ahead of the deadline. That evening, after a long day at school and then a four-hour shift at his job, Sam thought about how he should begin working on his project. His mind immediately went into over-drive and began to review all the questions still to be answered, the work to get done, and the time it would take to complete this project—and soon he felt exhausted. He just didn't have it in him to start the project and decided to get into bed, get a good night's sleep, and regroup in the morning. After a couple of weeks of the same pattern, Sam was beginning to feel he was in an impossible situation. He was already halfway into his semester, and he had barely made a dent on the project. He didn't know how to get himself out of the mess, so he decided to withdraw from the class to avoid having a failing grade on his record.

Noah, too, felt a wave of relief upon hearing that the majority of the coursework would not be due until the end of the semester, but he also felt a subtle hint of dread. He knew it would take a ton of discipline to work on the project a bit at a time throughout the semester so that he didn't end up desperate and scrambling as the due date approached. Noah was well aware of his tendency to procrastinate, so he tried to frame this project as an opportunity to rewire his brain to become more adept at "just doing it" instead of putting off whatever was too difficult and stressful. In order to break his old habits and create more effective new habits, he decided to set up an appointment with a student services learning specialist. Together, they sat down and created a detailed plan that outlined all the elements of the project and a schedule for when he should aim to complete each part. He realized that creating a solid plan was only a small portion of the battle; he still had to get the work done. He noticed his brain taunting him with the same old thoughts: "You still have so much time" and "You're too tired to do that right now. Take a break. You can work on it later." It was a struggle and sometimes he went back to his procrastinating ways. Other times, though, he was able to keep at it and work his newly discovered "just do it" muscle. He couldn't deny that something was different. It was getting easier to push forward despite all his brain's protests and complaints. It still took all the effort he could muster to put in an hour of work when every cell in his body wanted to relax, watch a show, and zone out. He realized he had a choice: he could push forward or take a break. The difference was that he was no longer on autopilot, instantly entering avoidance mode as soon as he felt stressed or overwhelmed.

You are no doubt all too familiar with the moral of this story. When life feels overwhelming or anxiety producing, it's perfectly natural to experience the desire to procrastinate and avoid contact with whatever is making you uncomfortable. What you may be less familiar with is that procrastination is anxiety's BFF. They go together better than PB and J or mac and cheese. Anxiety causes you to want to procrastinate, and procrastination then causes you to feel more anxious. Round and round you go, in what can feel like an endless cycle of fear and avoidance. But the good news is that you can rewire your brain to have a stronger "just do it muscle." Just like Noah, you too will soon be the proud owner of a brain that procrastinates and avoids less and is more readily able to face challenging tasks head-on.

☞ What's the main difference between how Sam and Noah handled the stress and procrastination urges associated with their final projects?

☞ How do you tend to handle situations when you feel overwhelmed and stressed and unclear how to proceed? Are you more similar to Sam or to Noah?

COMMON AVOIDANCE AND PROCRASTINATION STRATEGIES

Review this list of common avoidance and procrastination strategies used by many of the teens we work with. Which ones do you most turn to when you're feeling stuck and overwhelmed?

- Completing less stressful/lower priority tasks such as cleaning or organizing

- Mentally reviewing all the reasons you're a disaster and how hopeless your situation is

- Perfectionism-related behaviors to try to prevent making any mistakes

- Reassurance-seeking behaviors to try to get "all will be okay" from others

- Self-medicating with drugs or alcohol

- Restricting food intake or overeating

- Oversleeping

- Excessive reliance on technology to distract yourself

- Trying to control and plan out all aspects of life

- Blaming or getting angry at others

- List making and compulsively reviewing and analyzing what next steps you need to take

THE HOOK OF PROCRASTINATION AND AVOIDANCE

As you probably realize, the urge to procrastinate and avoid is incredibly hard to resist. The desire to limit distress and maximize comfort is a strong drive hardwired into the brains of all animals, including humans. It goes against survival instincts to do anything other than attempt to minimize discomfort. Isn't it a good idea to move your hand away from a hot stove? Of course it is!

Unfortunately, when it comes to emotional pain, the strategy of avoiding discomfort backfires and leads to more suffering. The behaviors you use to distance yourself from uncomfortable feelings reinforce your brain's belief that you're in danger. Why else would you be running from something? And as you now know, when your amygdala determines that you're in danger, it will sound the alarm and you'll experience more anxiety. So, if you want to feel less anxious, stop procrastinating and move forward instead.

Like all muscle groups, the mental circuitry that manages your ability to maneuver your way through overwhelming, stressful aspects of life can be strengthened with practice. By repeatedly practicing taking that next step forward rather than freezing or retreating, you'll rewire your brain to see you as competent and resilient instead of weak and fragile.

YOUR "JUST DO IT" MENTAL CIRCUITRY

A specific area of the brain called the *dorsal anterior cingulate cortex* (DACC) gets activated when you're flexing your "just do it" mental muscles and proceeding forward through overwhelming, stressful terrain. The DACC is part of the PFC network, connecting with other brain structures (including your amygdala) to get important information about the situation you're in and then help your body take appropriate action.

Research looking at brain scans tells us that procrastinators who don't regularly use their "just do it" circuitry tend to have larger amygdalae and weaker connections between the amygdala and DACC. This means they may feel more anxious and overfocus on the discomfort they feel when completing tasks. When you don't activate your "just do it" circuitry, there are more and more situations getting labeled by your amygdala as DANGER, leading to more and more anxious thoughts and feelings. Research also tells us that chronic procrastinators are more likely to feel low energy, low self-confidence, and symptoms of depression. Without exercising your "just do it" circuitry, the cycle of anxiety and avoidance continues, and you might end up finding yourself avoiding situations that you used to power through or even enjoy in the past.

Your Brain in "Just Do It" Mode

Fortunately, procrastinators are not doomed to chronic "stuck-ness." Thanks to neuroplasticity, you can rewire your brain to have stronger connections between the amygdala, PFC, and DACC. We know from research that the stronger these connections are, the better you'll be able to "just do it"—to reason, plan, and organize your way through overwhelming and stressful situations. Once you start consistently activating your "just do it" circuitry, you'll begin to notice how much easier it is to move through tasks. It will soon become second nature to quickly move past overwhelmed feelings and get to work.

Held Hostage by Your Thoughts

The teens we work with often express shame and despair as they discuss all the "simple" tasks and life requirements they can't seem to complete. For example, in a recent session, Noah was describing how he needed to replace his lost driver's license, yet whenever he thought about the steps he'd have to go through, he got so overwhelmed that he immediately engaged in mind-numbing distractions on his phone to calm himself down. Noah then expressed frustration and self-loathing at his "inability to deal with life." He instantly felt perplexed and exasperated by his difficulty completing even the most basic tasks, saying, "It shouldn't be such a big deal. What's wrong with me that I can't even get it together to replace my license? How am I ever going to make it as an adult? At this rate, I'm going to end up homeless."

When we talked further, we were able to uncover underlying beliefs that increased Noah's feelings of stress and anxiety. We tried an exercise where we had Noah think about his license for a few moments and then mindfully observe the flurry of thoughts that immediately surfaced. Noah was then able to see just how complicated and frightening the task of obtaining a new license was in his mind. Over a one-minute period, Noah had all these thoughts:

- What if when I show up to apply for my license I don't have all the right information and then I have to find another time to go back?

- What if I have to take the written exam again?

- This is so annoying.

- Life is too hard.

- I'll need at least a half day to work on this, but I have so much work that I don't have that kind of time to spare.

- If I just took care of this months ago, I wouldn't be in this mess.

- There must be something wrong with me that I can't do anything right.

- If anyone knew what a mess I truly am, they'd never want to be friends with me.

- I'm pathetic and not equipped for life.

All these thoughts that nibbled away at his peace of mind surfaced so rapidly that he wasn't even aware of what lay below his feelings of dread. All he knew was that this was a task that he desperately wanted to avoid.

Upon completing this exercise, Noah was able to cut himself some slack. He was starting to understand that his tendency to procrastinate was not due to being incompetent and lazy, but instead, because his brain was always trying to avoid the discomfort of being bombarded with negative thoughts.

COMMON THINKING ERRORS THAT LEAD TO PROCRASTINATION AND AVOIDANCE

Anxious thinking has a tendency to be catastrophic (assuming the worst will happen), rigid (believing there is only one way to see a situation), and narrow (homing in on details instead of the big picture). In fact, research has shown that people who have a tendency to procrastinate often engage in anxious thinking patterns that go hand in hand with high levels of emotional distress and nervousness about moving forward due to fear of making a mistake.

When you buy into your catastrophic thoughts about how bad or dangerous an upcoming challenge will be, you're increasing your emotional suffering:

Suffering = Built-in pain of a challenge + Catastrophic reaction to the challenge

Yes, many life tasks may be uncomfortable, unpleasant, and boring, but they're rarely as difficult or as painful as your catastrophic thoughts predict they will be.

These common thinking traps can lead you to feel overwhelmed and paralyzed by fear. Noticing your catastrophic thoughts, rather than immediately buying into them, is the first step in switching gears and viewing a situation more accurately.

All-or-Nothing Thinking

Take a moment to imagine your emotional reaction if you had to sort the clothes on your bedroom floor, putting away what was clean and running a load of laundry for what was dirty.

Next, imagine your emotional reaction if you had to go home tonight and dust, vacuum, wipe down all surfaces, and organize everything that was out of place in every single room.

Which task feels more overwhelming? Which task would you more strongly want to avoid?

People who tend to procrastinate and avoid often believe that the only way to give themselves credit for making progress is to complete the whole task. If you have a tendency to engage in all-or-nothing thinking, it's likely difficult for you to tolerate partial completion of tasks. When your mind reviews what needs to get done, it doesn't offer you a manageable and appropriately scaled assignment; instead it runs through the entire list of all elements and sub-elements of a task in excruciating detail. Who wouldn't be exhausted and overwhelmed after mentally reviewing every single aspect of every task there is in life?

Perfectionism

Take a moment to imagine your emotional reaction to having to write a three-paragraph essay on: "What would you wish for if you were granted one wish?" In this scenario, the only consequence of this assignment is that you'll learn more about yourself and what you want your life to be like.

Next, imagine your emotional reaction to having to write the same essay but this time, depending on how good it is, you'll either go to a great college, get a great job, and have a great life, *or* go to a terrible college, get a terrible job, and have a terrible life.

Which task feels more overwhelming? Which task would you more strongly want to avoid?

The fear of how getting something wrong might impact your future can lead to feeling like you're walking on a tightrope with no safety net. If you have perfectionistic thoughts, you'll likely think that any misstep can lead to disaster. This thinking pattern came in handy back when a caveman who mistook a snake for a branch, or a poisonous berry for a healthy treat, could face catastrophe. But in modern life, this extreme fear of making a mistake often provides an inaccurate analysis of the danger and negative consequences of simply getting something wrong. Engaging in "perfection or bust" thinking can lead you to feel trapped and terrified of proceeding.

Intolerance of Uncertainty

Take a moment to imagine your emotional reaction to two different challenges. The first is to walk through a maze with a guide encouraging you to move forward, telling you that all you need to do is put one foot in front of the other and the rest will work itself out. The second is to walk through a maze with a guide telling you that before you take any steps forward, you need to know the entire layout and be clear about where each turn of the maze will take you.

Which task feels more overwhelming? Which task would you more strongly want to avoid?

If you're intolerant of uncertainty, you feel as though you need to know and understand all aspects of a situation before moving forward. When life seems unclear, you'll often feel overwhelmed and tend to compulsively review and analyze, rather than learning by doing. If you always need to understand how a situation will unfold before you're willing to risk taking the next step, it becomes nearly impossible to make progress toward achieving your goals.

MOVING FROM "AVOID DOING IT" TO "JUST DO IT" THINKING

You can't change that your brain will occasionally be overzealous in its application of anxious thinking patterns to determine whether you're safe or in danger. But what you can change is how you relate to these thoughts. You can either take them at face value and believe they're accurate, or you can build upon the mindfulness practice introduced in chapter 3 and follow these steps:

1. Observe when anxious thinking patterns surface.

2. Challenge inaccurate assessments made by your anxious thoughts.

3. Disengage from anxious thoughts and bring your attention back to the current moment.

🔖 or 💻
Exercise #21: Observe and Disengage from Anxious Thoughts

Useful for: Rewiring a brain that gets stuck in overthinking.

Time needed: Five to ten minutes daily for one week

You can use your journal to complete this exercise or download the worksheet at http://www.newharbinger.com/43768, where you'll also find a completed sample.

For one week, practice noticing when you're having the urge to procrastinate. Start by writing down the task you'd like to avoid. Next, rate your anxiety on a scale from 1 to 10. Write down all the anxious thoughts that surface and, finally, include what kind of thinking error your mind is engaging in.

As you're doing this throughout the week, try to notice any patterns. People tend to have particular thoughts and types of thoughts that happen often and regularly. Are there any specific thoughts you notice creeping up more frequently than others? If so, write them down, and be on the lookout for them in the future.

For each of the scenarios you've written down, spend a few moments coming up with a more realistic interpretation. Imagine you're a lawyer trying to make your case to a judge and jury, and your argument must be based on facts. What statements would be accepted into the court record? Is not getting an A on a project enough evidence that you'll never succeed in life?

After you practice challenging your anxious thoughts and providing a more balanced assessment of the situation at hand, rate your anxiety level once more.

How Is This Exercise Rewiring Your Brain?

Rewiring your brain to engage in "just do it" thinking takes hard work and commitment to the lifelong practice of observing and challenging anxious thoughts as they surface. With practice, you're strengthening the connections in your brain so you get better at (1) noticing these automatic anxious thoughts, and (2) challenging them with more helpful and realistic thoughts that get you moving. You'll notice it's easier to "just do it" when your amygdala doesn't take your anxious thoughts so seriously, and instead has a better grasp on helpful and rational thoughts from your PFC.

STRENGTHEN YOUR "JUST DO IT" MENTAL CIRCUITRY

In addition to challenging your brain when it's engaging in anxious thinking errors, it's also critical to engage in targeted mental-strength training exercises that enhance your "just do it" circuitry. To rewire your brain to have a stronger "just do it" circuitry, you'll need to (1) assess your baseline functioning, (2) create a plan that specifies which exercises to practice and when to practice them, and (3) if you hit a roadblock and are unable to complete an exercise, identify the obstacles and revise your plan accordingly.

📱 or 💻
Exercise #22a: Where Are You Now?

Useful for: Rewiring a brain that needs help setting goals for what it wants in life.

Time needed: Ten minutes

You can use your journal or download the worksheet (with a sample completed version) at http://www.newharbinger.com/43768.

Consider your values—the areas of life that are most important to *you*—and rate how important each is on a scale of 1 to 10. Next, consider how much time and energy you actually channel into these areas, and rate how much you've been accomplishing in the past month, again on a scale of 1 to 10. The gap between what's important to you and what you're accomplishing is likely filled with anxiety, stress, and fear. For top priority aspects of your life where you feel stuck, identify one or two specific goals for yourself.

📖 or 💻
Exercise #22b: Create a Master Task List

Useful for: Rewiring a brain that gets overwhelmed by too many to-dos.

Time needed: Ten minutes

Again, you can use your journal or download the worksheet at http://www .newharbinger.com/43768.

Create a master task list to store and organize to-dos based on values and goals you identified in the previous exercise. For each item, determine its priority (low, medium, high) as well as how much time you'll need (a short, medium, or long amount). Update this list on an ongoing basis with new tasks as they surface.

And be careful that your to-do list does not become yet another procrastination strategy. Many teens we work with create endless lists of all the tasks they need to complete and wonder why this approach isn't working for them. Placing an item on a to-do list that isn't anchored in a specific day and time is no more helpful than ignoring the task altogether. In fact, it can actually be harmful, as it tricks the brain into believing it's accomplishing something and creates a short-term sense of relief—when in fact no progress is actually being made. Later in this chapter, you'll practice transforming your task list into a clear, defined weekly plan.

Setting Yourself Up for Success

Much like a strength-training plan, it's critical to start rewiring your brain slowly in order to set yourself up for success. If you haven't done any arm workouts for years, and you go to the gym and try to bench hundred-pound weights, you'll either make no progress or hurt yourself in the process. The same is true of strengthening your "just do it" circuitry. If you've been spending the majority of your time lately in procrastination land, it's unlikely that tomorrow you're going to be ready and able to engage in nonstop action mode. It's much healthier to provide yourself with a small win rather than another example of your inability to meet goals.

Smart Scheduling

It takes upfront planning to prioritize what needs to be done and when. It's critical to create a schedule that identifies a time block for working on each task you hope to accomplish. We recommend some kind of calendar system—either a planner or on your phone—where you can add each task as an appointment, with alerts if you use your phone. By doing this, you enhance your accountability for completing the task. It also forces you to think through how long the task will take to complete, instead of unrealistically under- or overestimating the time requirements.

An additional skill required to enhance your "just do it" circuitry is learning how to set clear, attainable, and defined goals for yourself. For example, instead of telling yourself you're going to "work on the paper tonight," assign yourself the more specific task of reading and outlining two research articles from eight to ten p.m. The key difference between assigning these tasks is that in the first situation, there's no way to tell when you have reached your goal. You can work on the paper for several hours and still feel like you haven't done enough.

In order to maximize the likelihood that you'll complete a self-assigned task, it's helpful to plan out when, where, and how long you're going to work on a task.

Deciding **When** to Work

Think about your natural rhythm. Some people are night owls and find themselves at their peak concentration levels in the evening, while others are most focused early in the day. What time of day is it easiest for you to think critically? Creatively? When do you have the most physical energy? When are your social skills best?

Think about the tasks you need to accomplish over the next week. Based on your natural rhythm, are some tasks better suited for you to do in the morning? Afternoon? Later in the day?

Because an object in motion stays in motion, try to get yourself up and moving and accomplishing as early in the day as possible. Even if you are more of a night owl, the earlier in the day you activate your "just do it" mental muscle, the better and the more likely this forward momentum will continue throughout the rest of your day.

Deciding **Where** to Work

Your brain is wired to pick up on a variety of sensory stimuli in the environment—that's how you learn to navigate and interact with the things and people around you. However, certain stimuli may easily distract you, or you may associate them with something other than getting work done. Research shows that a messy workspace can make it more difficult for you to focus on tasks, but you can create a space that sets you up for success. It's also helpful to surround yourself with go-getters who are getting their own work done, since research points to the idea of learning by watching others.

Quick changes like these can help you reboot your brain so it can operate in a less distracted and more effective processing mode:

- Move your phone out of the room.

- Log out of apps and sites that you have a tendency to get lost in.

- Get dressed before starting your work (rather than attempting to get your work done while you're still in pajamas).

- Work at a library, or your favorite coffee shop where other people are doing work.

- Work outdoors on a nice day.

Deciding How Long to Work

It's fine and often helpful to ask others how long they estimate a task should take; this can be especially helpful if you tend to be a perfectionist. Imagine you were spending an hour a night annotating a bibliography, then checked in with your teacher, who told you that it shouldn't take more than fifteen minutes and gave you some helpful tips to move through the task more swiftly.

Some tasks take more brainpower, making it harder to work for more than an hour without taking a break or switching gears such as writing a paper. Other tasks are less mentally taxing but more physically demanding, such as mowing the lawn or folding laundry. When possible, create a balance between mentally taxing and physically taxing tasks.

Be sure to take active breaks, such as getting up for water; going for a brief, brisk walk; or doing ten jumping jacks and five yoga stretches, rather than getting on your phone or using other technology. Many people have a hard time stopping once they get going, but working without a break reinforces all-or-nothing thinking and increases burnout. And it will make it more stressful to reengage once you finally stop because your brain will have unrealistic expectations of what it needs to accomplish.

Exercise #22c: Create Your Weekly "Just Do It" Brain Workout Plan

Useful for: Rewiring a brain that needs help mapping out time to get things done.

Time needed: To be completed over the couse of a week.

Based on the task list you created in the previous exercise, it's time to create a schedule of what you will be accomplishing for the next week.

- Review the tasks you labeled both high priority and short in terms of time needed.

- Open whatever calendar you prefer to use (paper or electronic).

- For the next seven days, find chunks of time to work on these tasks. Try to dedicate one to two hours a day to completing these tasks for the first week of this plan.

- As you move through your day, if there is a task you didn't get to, find a new day and time to reschedule it for.

- Consider each task a critical appointment you're making with yourself and stick with it.

How Are These Exercises Rewiring Your Brain?

By sorting out where you are now and prioritizing tasks to get to where you want to be, you're activating your PFC with rational and productive thinking. Your mountain of to-dos that usually freaks out your amygdala will no longer feel impossible to conquer. Uncomfortable feelings of dread can be defused when you simply start planning and prioritizing tasks, even when doing that feels impossible. Once you start activating your "just do it" circuitry on a consistent basis, you'll begin to notice how much easier it is to move through tasks. Your rational PFC thoughts will notify your amygdala that this seemingly large to-do list isn't impossible, threatening, or so dangerous that it needs to be avoided. Just as the more experience your amygdala gets with sitting through the discomfort and building connections to your helpful PFC, the more frequently you work your "just do it" muscles, the stronger they will get. Soon, it'll become easier for your amygdala to quickly move past anxious feelings and get to work.

COMMON ROADBLOCKS

When you hit a roadblock and you're not able to complete a required life task, *do* identify any obstacles that proved difficult for you to overcome, and revise your plan accordingly. *Don't* beat yourself up or give up. The most common obstacles identified by teens we work with are (1) lack of focus and commitment, (2) an unclear link between your tasks and your values, and (3) a feeling that doing these tasks is boring and tedious.

Lack of Focus and Commitment

If you were lost in a jungle, it wouldn't be helpful to focus on only one tree. Instead, it would be more effective for your brain to take in as much information as possible regarding this potentially threatening situation and to assess if danger is lurking to your left or to your right, from above you or below you. But when you're safe and sound and simply trying to work on, say, a school project, this operating state of scanning and reviewing for new information is inefficient and utterly frustrating.

When your anxious brain is pulling you in so many different directions and pointing out all the upcoming work you need to somehow get done, it can be difficult to stay focused on the task at hand. This scanning mental state often leads people to engage in task-switching behaviors. Task switching means deciding to work on one item and then having a thought such as *There's something else more important I should be working on*, then listening to this thought, stopping the current task, and beginning work on another task. Soon after switching tasks, another *I'm working on the wrong thing* kind of thought surfaces, which you believe, leading to initiating a new task. Round and round you go, starting many tasks but completing few to none.

You can rewire your brain to proceed forward and complete the task at hand by engaging in commitment exposures. Commitment exposures simply entail deciding what you're going to do, putting on mental blinders, and working on the task you assigned yourself. This requires practicing how to tolerate but not give in to thoughts that tell you doing something else would be a better use of your time.

An Unclear Link Between Your Tasks and Your Values

When the going gets tough and you want to quit, tap into your power-packed values to propel you forward. Research tells us that we're more motivated to engage in tasks that align with our values. When you're feeling motivated and can identify your values driving a task, your brain is getting a healthy dose of dopamine in the reward and motivation centers within the PFC. One study found higher levels of dopamine in those who were motivated to get tasks done, in contrast to those who tended to drag along doing tasks. Another way values helps enhance motivation is by increasing your brain's flexibility to move through old patterns of resistance and avoidance. And a bonus: when you act according to your values, research shows that it can help you feel more satisfied in your life, beyond just feeling less anxious.

Imagine that tomorrow morning you need to wake up at four, carry a heavy item, drive for an hour, wait in a long line, have strangers harshly ask you a series of questions, and then sit for another two hours. How motivated do you feel to engage in this series of behaviors?

Next, imagine that you need to wake up at four in order to head to the airport to embark on your dream adventure. How motivated would you be to engage in each of those same behaviors? If you weren't trying to get somewhere that mattered to you, why would you want to wake up at four and head to the airport to deal with all the hassles of travel?

When you lose track of how completing to-do list items moves you in the direction of your life goals, it can feel pointless and a waste of energy to deal with these tasks. Why wake up early and repetitively lift metal objects and get on a machine and run in place if you don't value fitness and wellness? It has to be worth it to channel your limited supply of energy into a task; otherwise, it's perfectly reasonable to choose to procrastinate and avoid.

So let's spend a few moments reminding yourself what's most important to you and what you want your life to be about. This exercise is similar to the first exercise you completed in this book, where you reminded yourself where you would be without anxiety. Now you're going to prompt your brain to reflect on what valued living means to you, and what makes it worth tolerating all the hard stuff that day-to-day living entails.

📖 or 💻

Exercise #23: What Does Valued Living Mean to You?

Useful for: Rewiring a brain that has trouble seeing the opportunities and exciting times ahead.

Time needed: Ten to fifteen minutes

When answering these questions, don't overthink. Just note what naturally bubbles up.

☞ What do you want your life to be about?

☞ What activities provide you with a sense of joy, vitality, and purpose?

☞ What activities do you engage in that leave you feeling empty and restless?

☞ If you could snap your fingers and make all anxiety disappear, what activities would you engage in? How would you fill your time? What would a perfect day entail?

Now that you've prompted yourself to consider what's most important to you, let's use this vision to help you push forward when the going gets tough and you want to avoid and procrastinate.

Using your journal or the worksheet you can download at http://www .newharbinger.com/43768, write a list of any tasks you assigned yourself in your weekly "Just Do It" plan and ended up not completing. In the next column, remind yourself why completing the task is important. In the third column, write down how it helps you live a life in line with your values. To remind yourself of the domains of life most important to you and your specific goals within them, you can refer back to exercise 22a.

The Act of "Doing" Feels Boring and Tedious

When you're working toward a long-term goal, your brain rewards you for making progress with a hefty serving of the feel-good neurotransmitter dopamine. Dopamine's job is to encourage you to act in order to achieve something good or avoid something bad. When you're doing the required subtasks that lead to your greater goal, it's easy for your brain to lose sight of how these microbehaviors connect with your life priorities. When your brain overlooks the connection between the tasks you need to accomplish and your values, you'll be shortchanged on receiving a boost of motivation-enhancing dopamine.

You can rewire your brain to reward you with small bursts of dopamine when you complete the tasks on your weekly "Just Do It" plan by making a game out of accomplishing them. Dopamine will flow as a result of your brain's positive reinforcement every time you "win" by completing a task.

Exercise #24: Gamify the Act of Accomplishing

Useful for: A brain that likes to compete and have fun when getting things done.

Time needed: To be completed over the couse of a week.

Make it a game to accomplish rather than procrastinate. Set a competition between team Just Do It and team Procrastinate. Using your journal (or a whiteboard, your phone, or your computer), set up a side for each team by drawing a line down the middle. Each time you accomplish something by fighting the urge to procrastinate, give team Just Do It a point. Each time you give in to the urge to avoid, give team Procrastinate a point. At the end of the week, tally up the points and determine who won. Also consider how close a game it was and what you learned about your opponent. Come up with one or two new strategies you will apply the following week to up your odds of winning.

Reward Yourself

Knowing that you will benefit in the long run from dealing with your tasks is motivating. Rewards—the stuff you want—are also motivating. Short-term rewards sweeten the deal and make the act of accomplishing your tasks less tedious and more enjoyable.

Think about recent jobs you've done (babysitting, chores, and so on). What motivated you to do these jobs? If you knew that you were going to get paid something (even a small amount), how likely would you be to show up? Most people need some compensation to be motivated, especially when it comes to completing difficult tasks.

When you're paid for a job, there's a clear reward structure. You may get paid by the hour or the task. Whatever the arrangement, you know before you begin the gig how you'll get paid. So how are you going to "pay" yourself for completing items on your weekly Just-Do-It plan? We recommend giving yourself a point for each task you complete. The following exercise will help you plan these out.

Exercise #25: Reward Yourself

Useful for: Rewiring a brain that needs something to look forward to after doing the hard work

1. Brainstorm a list of dream rewards. Do you fantasize about seeing your favorite band perform but don't have the funds for a ticket? Put it on the list. Would you love to upgrade your phone for a newer version? Put that down as well. Don't let practical realities get in the way of your list. Dream big!

2. For each item, decide how many "just do it" points it will take to earn it. For example, one teen put earning a pair of his dream sneakers on his reward list and assigned himself 250 points to obtain them.

3. Next, talk to trusted family members and see if they can sponsor you in this mission. Perhaps they would be eager to put money into a pot to help you get paid for your hard work.

4. Decide how you'll track the points you earn. For example, some teens we know keep track of their points on a chart they post on their family's refrigerator to remind their family of the progress they're making. Others track their points in a notebook or create a note for point tracking in their phone. In addition, there are tons of great apps for tracking desired habits

and healthy behaviors. It doesn't matter how you choose to track your points. What matters is that you do it.

5. Don't just think about rewarding yourself for working your "just do it" muscle; when you have earned enough points, truly reward yourself!

How Are These Exercises Rewiring Your Brain?

To help motivate you, your brain needs helpful reminders of *why* you would put forth effort and proceed despite other unhelpful, overwhelming messages from your amygdala. And sometimes the reason is so that you can reward yourself for your hard work (either with a "just do it" point or a special treat). These reminders and rewards help your PFC see the bigger picture and realize that it *actually wants* to get the task done, even though it may feel awful in the moment. The more you cue up reminders of your values and immediate rewards, the more your dopamine levels increase your motivation, and the better your PFC can shift attention away from panic and onto your important goals.

KEY TAKEAWAYS

Strengthening your "just do it" muscles is just like strengthening any other muscle. It takes frequent reps and consistent practice. And when building up muscle mass, there's no way to get the "gain" without some element of "pain." You'll soon find that it gets easier and easier to move past your brain's resistance. Once your brain catches on that you mean business, it will quiet down and conserve its energy for a battle it can actually win. The more you do, the easier it gets to do more.

CHAPTER 9

Rewire Your Brain to Be Confident

Prom was approaching, and Katie and Stephanie were shopping together for dresses. Neither had gone to prom before, and they weren't sure what to expect. As they browsed the aisles, Katie chose a number of dresses she thought would be fun to wear. Some were long, some short. Some were super trendy, and others more classic. Stephanie, meanwhile, stuck entirely to styles she thought were "safe" based on her extensive time spent scrolling through social media and looking at prom dresses that older girls from their school had worn.

In the dressing room, Katie burst out laughing at the first dress she tried on. It looked hideous, she remarked, snapping a photo to make their friends laugh later. She tried on a few others before settling on a light-blue dress. It was tighter than she thought she'd be comfortable wearing, but she felt confident in it and thought she looked pretty great.

Stephanie, on the other hand, was near tears. Each time she put on a dress she was overwhelmed by imagining how other people would see her. Would they think she looks too sexy? Not sexy enough? Like she's trying too hard? Like she's totally out of touch with what's cool? What if someone more popular picked the same dress? Finally, Stephanie chose a dress, but she was so caught up in trying to anticipate how other people would react that she wasn't even sure if she liked it herself. Each day until prom, she worried about how she'd look on the big night, and whether she had made the right choice.

The moral of this story is that Stephanie has a tendency to view her own experiences through other people's eyes, and this habit chips away at her confidence. Rather than doing things for herself, she's constantly trying to anticipate how others will judge what she does. Katie, by contrast, focuses more on her own desires, and as a result not only feels more confident but actually appears more confident to others—in turn earning more of their respect.

PERSPECTIVE TAKING AND THE BRAIN

Your brain has a wonderful ability to take perspective—that is, to see things through other people's eyes. Empathy, which includes perspective taking and emotional understanding for others, is often viewed as a strength that can help us form meaningful friendships and relationships with people. In your brain, empathy activates the nucleus accumbens and a part of the PFC, areas that are linked to reward and thinking skills. The ability to shift your thinking about other people's thinking—that's a thinking skill. Research has also found that the stronger the connections between a part of your PFC and the area of your brain where the temporal and parietal lobes meet, the more you're able to empathize and understand social interactions.

One more area in your brain plays a big role in understanding others' distress. *Mirror neurons*, in the area of your brain responsible for motor movements, are activated when you feel upset for others. Your mirror neurons mimic others' behaviors and emotions, and that's why it seems like you now feel their distress.

Some words of caution: sometimes experiencing too much of others' distress can lead to less clarity and confidence in yourself. And research has shown that feeling too overwhelmed by others' emotions can reduce your ability to be empathic. You may become more focused on your own distress, missing out on important social cues that could strengthen your relationships.

Exercise #26: Take a Social-Media Freeze (or at Least a Chill)

Useful for: Rewiring a brain that is obsessed with other people's perspectives.

Time needed: To be completed over the couse of weeks or months.

Over the years, we've noticed an increase in the number of teens who come to us saying they can't stop thinking about how other people view them. This might be due to an increase in the use of social media, which offers a constant stream of images of other people's (seemingly perfect) lives, as well as immediate feedback (such as likes or double-tap hearts) on the images you post of yourself. When these teens cut back on social media—or better yet, take a break entirely—their confidence tends to go way up, and their anxiety way down.

Let's take a story from Allie, one of the teens we worked with. During her senior year, Allie dated Chris for about five months before he ended the relationship. Allie was devastated and felt "left behind," yearning for the life she had with Chris. She checked his social media daily, eventually finding out he had a new girlfriend. Allie would stare at photos of the two of them, trying to understand what qualities this girl had that she didn't. As she moved through her days, she constantly compared herself to Chris's new girlfriend, and wondered what the two of them would think of Allie if they suddenly ran into her. One day, Allie logged in to see a stunning photo of Chris and his new girlfriend at the top of a mountain they had hiked, hugging each other and beaming. Chris's aunt had commented on the photo: "Sooooo excited for you!!!" Allie's heart sank. What was going on? It sure looked like they had big news. Allie thought to herself, *If only I were as lovable as she is* …. She continued to feel anxious and insecure.

A year later, Allie would learn through a friend that Chris and his girl-friend had broken up only two weeks after that photo was taken. At the time of the hike, they had apparently been having huge fights. Allie was stunned: the photo made it look like there was no way Chris and his now-ex-girlfriend were headed for anything but marriage. That photo had haunted her so much, chipping away at her confidence as she compared herself to the seemingly perfect ideal of their relationship. What if she had just never exposed herself to that photo at all?

Since that time, Allie has gone on several social-media "freezes," taking total breaks from checking any account. She's found that doing so makes life a whole lot easier. She doesn't think nearly as much about other people, her confidence has gone up, and her anxiety has gone down. But taking a break from social media is incredibly hard to do. Logging in can feel almost like an addiction. So what are the key steps to taking a freeze (a total break where you don't log in at all) or at least chilling your use (limiting it, for example, by blocking some people who cause you particular anxiety)?

First, define your plan by writing down answers to these questions in your journal:

- Which social media accounts do I want to take a break from?

- Am I taking a freeze or chilling my use?

   (We strongly advocate taking a freeze, as we find almost no one has the willpower to steer clear of certain content once they log into social media.)

- If I'm taking a freeze, do I want to deactivate my account or just not log in?

   (Some people choose to deactivate, at least temporarily; most social media sites will let you reactivate at any time. Others leave their accounts going, but just don't log in. If you take the second approach, we strongly recommend that you delete the app from as many of your devices as possible so that you don't get tempted.)

- How long will my break last?

   (Some people plan on just a couple of weeks while they're working through something especially challenging, like a breakup, and others go for a full year. To begin, we recommend three months. Just like an addiction, there will be an initial period where you'll crave logging in. However, this will pass, and most teens report actually feeling bored by social media when they finally go back. You want to get to this point, but it's impossible to do until you're past the "craving" phase.)

Try to find a friend to go on the social-media freeze (or chill) with you. It's way easier to do if you're accountable to someone else, and our teens usually say it's fun to discuss the experience with a friend. Alternatively, you can just let a friend or family member know about your goals and update them occasionally.

Whatever approach you decide on, remember to set clear goals. Note your freeze or chill end date in your calendar, and then get out there and enjoy living life outside of social media! We bet you'll feel much better once you do.

How Is This Exercise Rewiring Your Brain?

Humans are wired to take in most information visually. Your brain processes tens of thousands of visual messages an hour. Most of the brain that takes in sensory information is dedicated to vision. In fact, one research study found that your memory for information you see or feel is much stronger than for what you hear. And visual information about social situations can leave a mark in your long-term memory, and trigger emotions.

Research has shown that the visual cortex and reward areas in the brain are activated when teenagers look at their own and others' pictures that have a lot of "likes." When you constantly overload your brain with visuals of highly liked social situations, your brain starts to compare your social life to the unrealistic images online. You evaluate yourself, your social life, your friendships (to name a few), and then it starts to *feel* like you're lower on the social pyramid than you really are. Your confidence might start to crumble the more you evaluate yourself as "less than" through these visual images. Most people forget to reality-check themselves: this visual is filtered and altered, and is the very best photo people have chosen to share with the world.

☞ *On a scale of 1 to 10, rate how much it's a priority for you to take a break from social media.*

Exercise #27: Stand by Yourself

Useful for: Rewiring a brain that easily becomes insecure in the presence of others.

It's easy to view the world through others' eyes when we're scrolling through social media. But what about when we're actually hanging out with other people and become so concerned with measuring up that it makes us feel insecure? One of the traps we see many teens fall into when they feel inadequate in the eyes of their peers is putting themselves down. Putting yourself down can range from obvious acts, like declaring that something you did/like/feel is stupid, to more subtle forms, like always agreeing with other people rather than voicing your own opinions. The good news is that even if you don't *feel* confident, simply *acting* confident is likely to earn you more respect—and, over time, make you genuinely feel more confident.

To get warmed up for this exercise, think back to the last time you were feeling insecure around other people. What are some of the behaviors you did to put yourself down? For example, did you immediately agree with things somebody else said? Did you try to apologize for yourself? Did you seek reassurance from your friends?

Now, think of a way that you could have stood by yourself in that moment instead. If you were agreeing with everything someone was saying, you might instead think of a single opinion of your own that you could have expressed. If you apologized to your friends for texting them too much, you could instead imagine yourself not apologizing at all, and changing the conversation to a new topic. If you were seeking reassurance from friends, for instance, that the dress you wore to a party wasn't embarrassing, you could imagine yourself instead confidently telling your friends one thing you liked about your dress. Whatever it is, take the time to truly visualize how you would stand by yourself if you could go back in time and change one thing.

Now, make a point to stand by yourself in real life once a day. This might be by refusing to apologize for yourself in a moment you would normally do so, or voicing an opinion when you would typically stay quiet.

It may feel awkward at first, but if you do it each day, we bet it'll become more and more natural. Other people will start to view you as confident, and they'll be less inclined to put you down. You probably know this in your heart already, but confident people gain respect from others. The thing you might not have realized is that even people who just *act* confident get more respect, too.

How Is This Exercise Rewiring Your Brain?

Research from brain imaging studies has found that thinking positively about yourself activates areas in the PFC and reward pathways in the brain. The more you allow yourself to act confident, the more practice you have with taking a risk, and the more your brain gets to experience the positive feelings that come with confidence. By strengthening its connections, your brain learns over time that acting confident makes you feel good about yourself. Your brain also sometimes mixes up the difference between things that are imagined and things that happen, so if you visualize and practice acting confident, it will store these memories to pump you up for the real event.

☞ *On a scale of 1 to 10, rate how much it's a priority for you to practice standing by yourself when around other people.*

KEY TAKEAWAYS

The less we view our own lives through other people's eyes, the more confident we will feel. One good way to do this is to cut down on social media by going on a social-media freeze or chill. Another method is to simply *act* confident around others by standing up for yourself, even if you don't feel confident at the time. Over time, the confidence will catch up. Sometimes you have to fake it 'til you make it.

CHAPTER 10

Rewire Your Brain to Maintain Its Gains

Two of the teens we worked with, Steve and Tim, learned the same skills to combat anxiety that we've taught you in this book. Life wasn't perfect or stress-free when they finished seeing us (as we've discussed, painful situations are a natural part of life!), but both had much lower anxiety than when they first started. They both described feeling like their "rewired" brains were less reactive to challenging situations that used to cause them stress, and that when anxiety and stress did arise, they had tools to navigate the difficult emotions and keep anxiety in check.

Steve was feeling so good, in fact, that as time went on he stopped thinking much at all about the skills he had learned. Rather than actively doing exercises to continue rewiring his brain, he just moved through his days, enjoying the lower levels of anxiety he was now feeling. This worked well enough for the first four months, until it came time for Steve to compete in a big tennis match. Suddenly, his anxiety levels skyrocketed. He tried in a frenzy to challenge negative biases, do mindfulness exercises, and apply other tools we had taught him. But just as it's hard for a tennis player to perform at peak level in a high-pressure match after not exercising for months, so too was it challenging for Steve to suddenly apply his tools at a stressful time after not "working out" his brain for so long. The tools helped some, but not nearly as much as they would have if Steve had kept up his rewiring practice and stayed in good mental shape all along.

Tim, meanwhile, made a point to keep up with the rewiring exercises he had learned with us long after his formal sessions ended. He made a list of his favorite skills, and each day used at least one, even if it was as small as challenging a single negative bias with an alternative explanation. He also practiced just sitting with anxiety, reminding himself that the feeling was temporary and that what he was experiencing was just a false alarm, instead of running away from the discomfort like he used to do. Every few months, he'd go back and review the full list of the skills he had learned and select a few he wanted to start using more frequently. Like Steve, Tim experienced spikes in anxiety that could feel strong and overwhelming. But unlike Steve, Tim had practiced applying his skills—and his brain was better wired to overcome anxiety when it did hit—so the negative feelings never came on as strong or lasted as long.

What's the moral of this final story? It's probably pretty obvious to you: keep up with your brain rewiring exercises! We often tell the teens we work with that you can't take a shower once and expect to stay clean forever. Instead, you need to shower every day (or, you know, most days) in order to stay clean. Similarly, reading this book once isn't going to rid you of anxiety forever. You hopefully feel better now that you've worked through it, just like you feel clean after taking a shower. But now it's up to you to stay "clean." In this last chapter, we'll guide you through the process of identifying the rewiring skills that will help you the most and coming up with a plan for using them.

MAINTAINING GAINS AND THE BRAIN

You might ask at this point: Wait, if I spent all this time rewiring my brain, why do I need to keep exercising? Aren't I rewired now? Think back to the beginning of this book where we talked about neuroplasticity—the wonderful, shapeable aspect of your brain. You've now learned how to take advantage of this cool process by rewiring your brain to overcome anxiety. Now, you have to "use it or lose it!" Your teenage brain is undergoing a lot of construction at the moment through a process called *synaptic pruning*. Unimportant information and wiring in your brain is weeded out. Practicing your new rewiring skills, however, will strengthen these neural pathways in your brain and signal to your brain that this is important wiring that needs to stay. In fact, a process called *myelination* in your brain increases the speed and strength of signals in your neural pathways. And what helps myelinate these pathways? Practice, practice, practice. Both repetition and quality of practicing new skills are essential for myelination to occur within your newly rewired pathways.

Just like any new skill you've learned, in order to keep it and get better at it, you must practice. Same goes for your newly rewired brain. If you don't keep up with these new habits that have started to rewire your brain, it will take longer for the new pathway to become the familiar one that your brain will so very much appreciate. The more you do the rewiring exercises that help you feel less anxious, the stronger this wiring becomes, and the easier it will be for your brain to use this neural pathway in the future.

HOW WE THINK MAINTAINING GAINS SHOULD GO VS. HOW IT ACTUALLY GOES

When Steve's tennis match was approaching and his anxiety started to go up, not only was he uncomfortable because he was feeling more anxious, but he was also freaked out to see his anxiety levels so high in a way he hadn't experienced since before he worked with us. One evening he screamed at his mom, "Everything is terrible! All that time I put into learning skills to rewire my brain didn't even work … here I am, back at square one. I'm going to lose my tennis match and be anxious forever!"

We can almost guarantee you that something like this will happen to you at some point. You'll feel better, then life will get hard—as it does!—and you'll be convinced you're back at square one. This has happened to almost every teen we've worked with, and we've all experienced it ourselves.

However, it's actually all a bit of a mental illusion. What do we mean by this? First, take a look at how most people imagine maintaining gains should look:

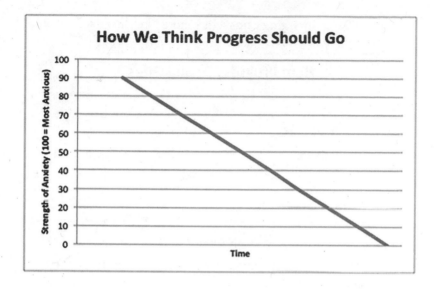

The "0–100" in that graph symbolizes how anxious you are, with 100 being the most anxious you've ever felt. "Time" just represents each day of your life. So basically, most people imagine that once they've learned skills to rewire their brains, their anxiety should go down more and more each day.

In reality, maintaining gains looks more like this:

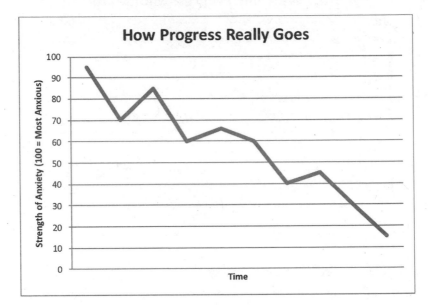

How Progress Really Goes

Strength of Anxiety (100 = Most Anxious)

Time

This graph is from an actual teen we treated, whose anxiety was at around a 95 when they first came to see us. You'll see that as time passed, their level of anxiety generally went down. For example, they rated their anxiety at about a 70 out of 100 a month after treatment. But then something happened: they approached finals, and their anxiety started to spike again, hitting about an 85. At that point, the teen had a bit of a meltdown in our office, telling us that everything was as "bad as ever," that they "weren't really better at all," and that they would "always" be anxious. You'll notice, though, that the anxiety didn't go up quite as high as it had been before, and critically *it went down again* as they stuck with their rewiring skills, hitting an even lower point than it had before. As you can see, they continued to face challenging times, but the spikes in anxiety went less and less high over time, and were fewer and farther between. Overall, their anxiety decreased, although on any given day there might be a spike.

When you're in one of those spikes, you will probably lose your perspective (and your cool) like Steve did, insisting that the anxiety is as high as it has ever been and that you haven't made any real progress. As one teen once told us, "If you run ten miles, you don't expect to suddenly be back at mile one." That's how it can feel when anxiety spikes. But if you track your symptoms over time, we'd bet you a hundred bucks that your anxiety peaks tend not to go as high as they used to, and that you recover more quickly from each spike. In other words, you aren't back at mile one at all. Recognizing that spikes will occur, and keeping track of the real picture of how progress looks, is critical to not getting thrown off track.

UPS, DOWNS, AND THE BRAIN

Your wonderful brain also likes to make things easy for you by doing what is most familiar; it will want to revisit that other pathway of old habits and heightened anxiety it's known for so long. And this is normal for your brain to do! Your brain will experience bumps in the road, and in times of panic it sometimes may go back to its old and trusted pathway. Remember that anxiety's sole purpose is to keep us safe. As you continue to rewire your brain so that it learns about false alarms, your hardwiring as a human might kick in and go into protection mode. Your new rewired patterns need practice to become stronger and needs these experiences in order for your amygdala to trust this new wiring. Even with newly learned skills, there will always be times when you feel anxious, because you're human and you'll encounter new and uncertain experiences in your life. But not every new experience will fill you with anxiety, thanks to your new rewiring skills.

When you do hit a bump, this is actually an especially powerful time to enhance your rewiring by applying your skills. You've now provided your brain with an opportunity for learning. In these moments, you need to put even more effort into practicing your rewiring skills, giving them extra attention and practice. Now your brain will have the experience of moving past this bump using the new rewiring skills, and not the old, unhelpful pathway.

WHEN TO GET MORE HELP

Before we jump into creating your personalized plan for continuing to overcome anxiety after you've finished this book, it's important to pause and reflect on when it's a good idea to get professional help outside of a book. Keep in mind that getting help is not any sort of sign of weakness or failure. Far from it! We firmly believe that *everyone* will benefit from therapy at some point in their life (we have all received it!), and that being able to recognize those points is an incredible skill that will make your life much easier. Think about it: If you had a mild sore throat, then sure, it would make sense to try to heal on your own. You might eat healthy foods and be sure to get extra sleep. But if that sore throat got especially severe, turning into a strep infection that required antibiotics, would it make more sense to continue trying to heal yourself, or to go to a doctor? Anxiety works the same way. When it gets too severe, recovery will be much faster with the help of a trained professional. So what are the signs you should seek therapy?

- You've finished this book and are still experiencing substantial anxiety. By "substantial," we mean on a scale of 0 to 10, where 10 is the highest level of anxiety, you're on average still experiencing 5 or above. It's getting in the way of your life in some ways, making it hard to sleep or do homework or socialize, or maybe it's just really unpleasant to feel. Either way, you could benefit from additional help if any of this is going on.

- Maybe your anxiety was so strong that it was hard to even start this book or do many of the exercises in it. If so, it would be a good time to get therapy. A trained therapist can help identify what is getting in the way of your progress and give you encouragement to fight your anxiety.

- You're having thoughts about hurting yourself or someone else. If this is happening, it doesn't make you a bad person. It's not shameful, but it's hard to live with and requires professional attention.

- You find that you're drinking or using drugs (including prescription medications in a way other than they were prescribed) in order to self-medicate or lower your anxiety.

Getting help can feel overwhelming but is often easier than you think. You might start by telling your school nurse or counselor that you're looking to see a therapist for anxiety or depression. They can help connect you to a therapist. You could show this chapter to your parents and explain that you'd like to see a therapist, or you can turn to the Internet. Organizations like the Anxiety and Depression Association of America have excellent resources, including listings of therapists who provide anxiety therapy (www.adaa.org).

MAKING A PERSONALIZED PLAN TO MAINTAIN YOUR GAINS

To maintain your gains from this book, it's important to set up a personalized plan for continuing to rewire your brain. Here, we'll lay out a simple process for identifying the skills you most want to continue practicing, knowing when to use these skills, and scheduling rewiring "booster" sessions that—much as the name suggests—will give you rewiring boosts to help ensure your long-term success overcoming anxiety.

Step 1: Identify the tools you value most.

What this step is helpful for: Making a short list of the tools from this book that you most want to continue practicing.

You might remember that at the end of many exercises, you completed a scale that looked like this example:

☞ *On a scale of 1 to 10, rate how much it's a priority for you to continue to work on establishing your own personal meditation practice.*

Go back through each chapter now and identify the tool you rated as the highest priority. If two or more were tied, pick just one for now. There will be chances to go back and use other tools later.

Next, use your journal to list your top-rated tools. You might jot down a few words to help yourself remember how to use the tool, as well as the corresponding page number from this book so that you can go back and quickly read about it in more detail in the future. Voilá! You've got the beginning of a road map for maintaining your gains.

Step 2: Identify the signs that it's time to use each tool.

What this step is helpful for: Remembering when to use your tools.

Next to each tool, write down a concrete sign or two that it's time to use that tool. For example, if you found that the 3-3-3 mindfulness exercise was especially powerful for helping you lower levels of physical anxiety when you started to feel the symptoms of a panic attack, you might write, "Use when starting to feel panic symptoms, like a pounding heart or racing thoughts." The more specific you can be, including warning signs like a pounding heart, the better.

Identifying signs that it's time to use a tool serves two main purposes. First, it provides you with a *plan* for facing the most anxiety-provoking situations in your life. Rather than entering stressful events feeling helpless, you will be armed with powerful strategies to manage your anxiety. Second, it gives you cues to help you *remember* to use your skills. If you can make a pounding heart into a sign to yourself to use the 3-3-3- mindfulness exercise, then you won't forget to practice that skill.

Related to that point, many of the teens we work with say that remembering to use their tools is one of the hardest parts of continuing to battle anxiety. It's easy, as Steve found out, to go on autopilot, failing to push yourself to continue rewiring your brain until you're faced with serious stress. To avoid this fate, we recommend putting this list of tools and signs that it's time to use them somewhere you will see regularly—maybe on your dresser, in a notebook, or scanned into your phone.

Step 3: Schedule booster sessions.

What this step is helpful for: Giving yourself boosts to continue fighting anxiety.

When we work with teens in person, we often schedule booster sessions for a few months after therapy is over. During the booster, they come in to discuss how their anxiety has been since the last session, review the full list of tools they had learned during therapy, and make decisions about which skills they'd like to focus on going forward.

We recommend something similar for you, our reader. Take out your calendar and make a note that says "Booster Session" for about three months from now. You might also note this page number in the book, so that you can easily find instructions for what to do during the booster session that you'll be holding with yourself and the book.

At that time, sit and reflect on how your anxiety levels have been. Looking back over the different chapters in this book, are there some areas where you've done especially well? Are there others where you could use more work?

Similarly, review the list of tools and signs to use each tool that you generated in steps 1 and 2. Going back over the tools in this book, do you want to make any changes to your list? In general, you want to keep on your list any tools that continue to be helpful to you, or that you forgot about but want to prioritize. You can remove any that haven't been helpful, or that have become so second nature that you no longer need to take space to remind yourself of them. Then, add any new tools from the book that you'd like to focus on over the next three months: maybe ones that have become especially relevant to your life now, or that were too hard before, but you feel ready to take on at this point.

When you're finished, make a note for another booster session in another three months. Continuing to check in with yourself and this book through regular boosters is a great way to make sure you maintain your gains.

Step 4: Live your life, not anxiety's life.

Congratulations on making it to the end of this book! Whether you dutifully practiced every exercise or skipped around and found just the tools you needed most in that moment, you've taken valuable steps toward rewiring your brain and overcoming anxiety. We hope that you'll take some time to set up a plan for continuing to stay in top mental shape, using the simple steps you just read about. More than anything, though, we hope that you'll enjoy getting out there and living your life!

KEY TAKEAWAYS

Progress isn't a straight line, but just 'cause you've hit a spike in anxiety doesn't mean you're back to square one. To maintain your rewired brain, identify the tools from this book that help you the most, along with the signs that it's time to use them. Schedule a booster session for a few months from now.

If there's one message we want to leave you with, it's this: Anxiety does not have to run your life. Don't give in to the fear, and don't be afraid to make mistakes and do the opposite of what anxiety tells you. Right on the other side of anxiety are some of the best experiences you will ever have in your life. You've got this!

References

Acevedo, B. P., E. N. Aron, A. Aron, M. D. Sangster, N. Collins, and L. L. Brown. 2014. "The Highly Sensitive Brain: An fMRI Study of Sensory Processing Sensitivity and Response to Others' Emotions." *Brain and Behavior* 4: 580–594.

Ahmed, S. P., A. Bittencourt-Hewitt, and C. L. Sebastian. 2015. "Neurocognitive Bases of Emotion Regulation Development in Adolescence." *Developmental Cognitive Neuroscience* 15: 11–25.

Banks, S. J., K. T. Eddy, M. Angstadt, P. J. Nathan, and K. L. Phan,. 2007. "Amygdala-Frontal Connectivity During Emotion Regulation." *Social Cognitive and Affective Neuroscience* 2: 303–312. doi: 10.1093/scan /nsm029.

Bengtsson, S. L., Z. Nagy, S. Skare, L. Forsman, H. Forssberg, and F. Ullén. 2005. "Extensive Piano Practicing Has Regionally Specific Effects on White Matter Development." *Nature Neuroscience* 8: 1148.

Bigelow, J., and A. Poremba. 2014. "Achilles' Ear? Inferior Human Short-Term and Recognition Memory in the Auditory Modality." *PloS One* 9: e89914.

Bramwell, K., and T. Richardson. 2018. "Improvements in Depression and Mental Health After Acceptance and Commitment Therapy Are Related to Changes in Defusion and Values-Based Action." *Journal of Contemporary Psychotherapy* 48: 9–14. doi:10.1007/s10879-017-9367-6.

Cheung, R. Y., and M. C. Ng. 2019. "Mindfulness and Symptoms of Depression and Anxiety: The Underlying Roles of Awareness, Acceptance, Impulse Control, and Emotion Regulation." *Mindfulness* 10: 1124–1135.

Clark, D. M., and A. Wells. 1997. "Cognitive Therapy for Anxiety Disorders." *Review of Psychiatry* 16: 1–9.

Cohen, N., D. S. Margulies, S. Ashkenazi, A. Schäfer, M. Taubert, A. Henik, A. Vilringer, and H. Okon-Singer. 2016. "Using Executive Control Training to Suppress Amygdala Reactivity to Aversive Information." *NeuroImage* 125: 1022–1031.

Davidson, R. J. 2002. "Anxiety and Affective Style: Role of Prefrontal Cortex and Amygdala." *Biological Psychiatry* 51: 68–80.

Etkin, A., T. Egner, and R. Kalisch. 2011. "Emotional Processing in Anterior Cingulate and Medial Prefrontal Cortex." *Trends in Cognitive Sciences* 15: 85–93. doi: 10.1016/j.tics.2010.11.004.

Gilboa-Schechtman, E., D. Erhard-Weiss, and P. Jeczemien. 2002. "Interpersonal Deficits Meet Cognitive Biases: Memory for Facial Expressions in Depressed and Anxious Men and Women." *Psychiatry Research* 113: 279–293.

Goldsmith, H. H., and K. S. Lemery. 2000. "Linking Temperamental Fearfulness and Anxiety Symptoms: A Behavior–Genetic Perspective." *Biological Psychiatry* 48: 1199–1209.

Hartline, D. K., and D. R. Colman. 2007. "Rapid Conduction and the Evolution of Giant Axons and Myelinated Fibers." *Current Biology* 17: R29–R35.

Hoyer, J., J. Čolić, G. Grübler, and A. T. Gloster. 2019. "Valued Living Before and After CBT." *Journal of Contemporary Psychotherapy*: 1–9. doi: 10.1007/s10879-019-09430-x.

Klimecki, O. M., S. Leiberg, M. Ricard, and T. Singer. 2013. "Differential Pattern of Functional Brain Plasticity After Compassion and Empathy Training." *Social Cognitive and Affective Neuroscience* 9(6): 873–879.

Kohn, N., S. B. Eickhoff, M. Scheller, A. R. Laird, P. T. Fox, and U. Habel. 2014. "Neural Network of Cognitive Emotion Regulation–An ALE Meta-Analysis and MACM Analysis." *NeuroImage* 87: 345–355.

Kral, T. R., B. S. Schuyler, J. A. Mumford, M. A. Rosenkranz, A. Lutz, and R. J. Davidson. 2018. "Impact of Short- and Long-Term Mindfulness Meditation Training on Amygdala Reactivity to Emotional Stimuli." *NeuroImage* 181: 301–313.

Neff, K. D., K. L. Kirkpatrick, and S. S. Rude. 2007. "Self-Compassion and Adaptive Psychological Functioning." *Journal of Research in Personality* 41: 139–154.

Pan, J., L. Zhan, C. Hu, J. Yang, C. Wang, L. Gu, et al. 2018. "Emotion Regulation and Complex Brain Networks: Association Between Expressive Suppression and Efficiency in the Fronto-Parietal Network and Default-Mode Network." *Frontiers in Human Neuroscience* 12: 70.

Pittman, C. M., and E. M. Karle. 2015. *Rewire Your Anxious Brain: How to Use the Neuroscience of Fear to End Anxiety, Panic, and Worry*. Oakland, CA: New Harbinger Publications.

Porges, S. W., J. A. Doussard-Roosevelt, and A. K. Maiti. 1994. "Vagal Tone and the Physiological Regulation of Emotion." *Monographs of the Society for Research in Child Development* 59: 167–186.

Raes, F. 2010. "Rumination and Worry as Mediators of the Relationship Between Self-Compassion and Depression and Anxiety." *Personality and Individual Differences* 48: 757–761.

Rauch, S. L., L. M. Shin, and C. I. Wright. 2003. "Neuroimaging Studies of Amygdala Function in Anxiety Disorders." *Annals of the New York Academy of Sciences* 985: 389–410.

Schlüter, C., C. Fraenz, M. Pinnow, P. Friedrich, O. Güntürkün, and E. Genç. 2018. "The Structural and Functional Signature of Action Control." *Psychological Science* 29: 1620–1630. doi: 10.1177/0956797618 779380.

Scult, M. A., A. R. Knodt, J. R. Swartz, B. D. Brigidi, and A. R. Hariri. 2017. "Thinking and Feeling: Individual Differences in Habitual Emotion Regulation and Stress-Related Mood Are Associated with Prefrontal Executive Control." *Clinical Psychological Science* 5: 150–157. doi: 10.1177/2167702616654688.

Swain, J., K. Hancock, A. Dixon, S. Koo, and J. Bowman. 2013. "Acceptance and Commitment Therapy for Anxious Children and Adolescents: Study Protocol for a Randomized Controlled Trial." *Trials* 14: 140. doi:10.1186/1745-6215-14-140.

Treadway, M. T., J. W. Buckholtz, R. L. Cowan, N. D. Woodward, R. Li, M. S. Ansari, R. Baldwin, A. N. Schwartzman, R. M. Kessler, and D. H. Zald. 2012. "Dopaminergic Mechanisms of Individual Differences in Human Effort-Based Decision-Making." *Journal of Neuroscience* 32: 6170–6176.

Welford, M. 2010. "A Compassion-Focused Approach to Anxiety Disorders." *International Journal of Cognitive Therapy* 3: 124–140.

Williams, L. M., J. M. Gatt, P. R. Schofield, G. Olivieri, A. Peduto, and E. Gordon. 2009. "Negativity Bias' in Risk for Depression and Anxiety: Brain-Body Fear Circuitry Correlates, 5-HTT-LPR and Early Life Stress." *NeuroImage* 47: 804–814.

Wolgast, M., and L. G. Lundh. 2017. "Is Distraction an Adaptive or Maladaptive Strategy for Emotion Regulation? A Person-Oriented Approach." *Journal of Psychopathology and Behavioral Assessment* 39: 117–127.

Young, K. S., A. M. van der Velden, M. G. Craske, K. J. Pallesen, L. Fjorback, A. Roepstorff, and C. E. Parsons. 2018. "The Impact of Mindfulness-Based Interventions on Brain Activity: A Systematic Review of Functional Magnetic Resonance Imaging Studies." *Neuroscience and Biobehavioral Reviews* 84: 424–433.

Debra Kissen, PhD, is CEO of Light on Anxiety CBT Treatment Center. Kissen specializes in cognitive behavioral therapy (CBT) for anxiety disorders, and has a special interest in the principles of mindfulness and their application for anxiety disorders. She is coauthor of *The Panic Workbook for Teens*, and is an active contributor to *HuffPost*, where she regularly shares information on the empirically supported treatment for anxiety and related disorders. Kissen is cochair of the Anxiety and Depression Association of America (ADAA) Public Education Committee. She often serves as a media psychologist, and is available for press inquiries.

Ashley D. Kendall, PhD, is a clinical psychologist who conducts NIH-funded research on mental health treatment for teens, and specializes in treating anxiety- and stress-related disorders in teens and adults. She received her PhD in clinical science from Northwestern University. Kendall is particularly interested in combining CBT with mindfulness-based techniques to help people overcome anxiety, stress, anger, and depression.

Michelle Lozano, LMFT, is a marriage and family therapist at Lutheran Social Services of Illinois, with placement at John H. Stroger, Jr. Hospital at Cook County in Chicago, IL. Lozano belongs to the ADAA, and the American Association of Marriage and Family Therapy. She has guest lectured at Loyola University Chicago, as well as The Graduate School at Northwestern University, on working with the patient's family system in therapy. Lozano provides family and group therapy to children and adolescents with chronic medical conditions in an effort to improve their emotional well-being and overall health. She is particularly interested in providing patients with the education and tools to become their own mental health coach to live more fulfilling lives.

Micah Ioffe, PhD, is a clinical psychologist who specializes in the treatment of youth anxiety disorders. She earned her PhD in clinical psychology from Northern Illinois University, with an emphasis on child and adolescent development. Ioffe utilizes both CBT and acceptance and commitment therapy (ACT) in her work with teens to help them move through anxious moments feeling empowered, fulfilled, and brave.

More ⏱Instant Help Books for Teens

An Imprint of New Harbinger Publications

A TEEN'S GUIDE TO GETTING STUFF DONE
Discover Your Procrastination Type, Stop Putting Things Off & Reach Your Goals
978-1626255876 / US $16.95

JUST AS YOU ARE
A Teen's Guide to Self-Acceptance & Lasting Self-Esteem
978-1626255906 / US $16.95

THE GRIT GUIDE FOR TEENS
A Workbook to Help You Build Perseverance, Self-Control & a Growth Mindset
978-1626258563 / US $16.95

THE INSOMNIA WORKBOOK FOR TEENS
Skills to Help You Stop Stressing & Start Sleeping Better
978-1684031245 / US $17.95

PUT YOUR WORRIES HERE
A Creative Journal for Teens with Anxiety
978-1684032143 / US $16.95

THE SOCIAL MEDIA WORKBOOK FOR TEENS
Skills to Help You Balance Screen Time, Manage Stress & Take Charge of Your Life
978-1684031900 / US $16.95

newharbingerpublications
1-800-748-6273 / newharbinger.com

(VISA, MC, AMEX / prices subject to change without notice)

Follow Us 📷 📘 🐦 ▶️ 📌 in

Don't miss out on new books in the subjects that interest you.
Sign up for our Book Alerts at **newharbinger.com/bookalerts**

Register your **new harbinger** titles for additional benefits!

When you register your **new harbinger** title—purchased in any format, from any source—you get access to benefits like the following:

- Downloadable accessories like printable worksheets and extra content

- Instructional videos and audio files

- Information about updates, corrections, and new editions

Not every title has accessories, but we're adding new material all the time.

Access free accessories in 3 easy steps:

1. Sign in at NewHarbinger.com (or **register** to create an account).

2. Click on **register a book**. Search for your title and click the **register** button when it appears.

3. Click on the **book cover or title** to go to its details page. Click on **accessories** to view and access files.

That's all there is to it!

If you need help, visit:

NewHarbinger.com/accessories

new harbinger
CELEBRATING
40 YEARS